Pelican Books
Playing Politics

Michael Laver was born in London in 1949 and
educated at Essex University. He then taught politics
at Queen's University, Belfast, and since 1973 has
been teaching politics at Liverpool University. His
previous publications include articles and
monographs on various aspects of politics, including
coalitions, party competition, electoral systems,
political loyalty, multinational corporations and
power, as well as lying, cheating and bluffing. He is
currently working on an analysis of strategic theories
of politics, and pursuing his interest in all aspects of
gaming.

Michael Laver

PLAYING
POLITICS

Penguin Books

Penguin Books Ltd, Harmondsworth,
Middlesex, England
Penguin Books, 625 Madison Avenue,
New York, New York 10022, U.S.A.
Penguin Books Australia Ltd, Ringwood,
Victoria, Australia
Penguin Books Canada Ltd, 2801 John Street,
Markham, Ontario, Canada L3R 1B4
Penguin Books (N.Z.) Ltd, 182–190 Wairau Road,
Auckland 10, New Zealand

First published 1979
Copyright © Michael Laver, 1979
All rights reserved

Made and printed in Great Britain by
Hazell Watson & Viney Ltd,
Aylesbury, Bucks
Set in Linotype Juliana

Contents

Acknowledgements

It would have been impossible to develop these games without access to a pool of tame players. To the many who tolerated the failures, and to some who made invaluable suggestions for improvement, I offer my warmest thanks. In particular, my 1977–8 Strategic Interaction group at Liverpool (Chris Watson, Mike Speakman, Jane O'Connell and Nick Bond) provided the stimulus to put the whole thing together. Chris contributed many valuable ideas to Chapter 3, and Mike did the same for Chapter 4. I made the mistakes.

Introduction

This is a book of games and a book about politics. I hope the games are fun to play, and I hope they can be enjoyed by people who don't care at all about politics. They do, however, have a serious purpose: each game is an attempt to capture one of the essential puzzles of the political process. Politics is not a game, of course; it is a serious business. Nevertheless, one important aspect of politics is *like* a game. What actually happens is usually the result of the calculated and calculating interaction between self-seeking political actors, be they private individuals, politicians, political parties, pressure groups, national governments or even whole alliances of countries. Calculated and calculating interaction is what games are all about. The purpose of this book is to distil some of the essence of these real political interactions and to represent them as simple games which the reader can play. The reason for doing this is not *just* so that people can have fun and not at all to suggest that politics is a trivial process. People might have fun and politics might be trivial but I hope that, by facing up to the simplified dilemmas which follow, people will be able to get a little bit more of a feel for some of the fascinating deviousness of real-world politics.

It is impossible to write a book of this nature without including quite a lot of political content. Purging the book of such content would make it sterile and boring. No doubt many readers will detect what they see as political bias or ideology in many of the comments I make. This too is inevitable, so it is as well to come clean about my own political persuasions. I am a cynic, and I am afraid that this is a cynical book. There is no doubt that it presents politics as a cynical process and politicians as cynical people. This is not as serious as it might seem, because the book is not about the great issues of politics. It is about the nitty gritty of getting your own way. Even idealists, if they are to be effective, must get their hands dirty from time to time. The games in this book are about how to do this well.

Some of the games are about getting into power, and the players are allowed to say and do almost anything to get there. Some of the games give the players immutable policies (call them ideals if it makes you feel better) which they must realize. However, all of the games are about means and not ends, and I do sincerely believe that, when it come to means, in politics anything goes. Thus the cut and thrust which is represented in the following pages is equally likely in the politics of a large capitalist corporation, a western liberal democracy or in the decision-making bodies of a socialist state. The ends, of course, will be very different, but the means can be uncannily similar.

The games are arranged in a sequence. They start, not with the easiest, but with the most primitive. They finish, not with the hardest, but with the most sophisticated. The first game is about politics without any political institutions at all. It has hardly any rules because the game is about making up the rules. It can end in chaos or order; that's its point. We start with a group of isolated individuals; each must cooperate with the others if any are to survive while each must beat the others in order to win. This is the starting point of politics, which can be thought of as a set of arrangements designed to increase social well-being by helping, or forcing, people to cooperate with each other. Most political arguments concern what we mean by social well-being, and which rules of the game are best designed to achieve it.

Once we have seen the ways in which politics might emerge, our attention turns to politicians. One solution, although by no means the *only* solution, to the problem of how to increase social well-being is to appoint a group of people to organize and coordinate our lives. Notable alternatives to this include anarchy, in which we try to coordinate our lives without interference from above, and dictatorship, in which all power to do this is vested in one person. One way out of the 'primitive politics' problem, however, especially when there are large numbers of players, is to appoint a representative to organize the cooperation which is necessary to extract resources from Nature. For the sake of argument, we will call this person a politician. Politicians must be rewarded for their efforts on our behalf, of course. For the sake of argument we will call these rewards spoils. Obviously one solitary politician is no solution at all to the problem since we would quickly have a dictator on our hands. When there are rich pickings to be had, we need not worry unduly about the dangers of ending up with only one politician. Many hopeful candidates will want to share a piece of the action, and will compete with each other to do so. The second game is therefore about competition between politicians for the spoils which are available when they take office. Each round represents a straight fight between an incumbent, who won the last election, and a challenger. The rest of the players are voters, who want to choose the leader who looks like producing policies which are as close as possible to the ones they prefer. The voters are in competition with each other to elect the leader whose programme is closest to the one they would most like. The politicians are in competition with each other for the spoils. They are also in competition with the electorate to sell a package which is attractive enough to get them elected, but which still allows them to make a profit. Aspiring leaders must build up sufficient credibility to convince the electorate to vote for them, bearing in mind that if they are too straightforward they will not be able to make a profit. The two primitive games therefore show us firstly how politics might help us by ordering our lives and secondly how politicians, for their own selfish reasons, can contribute to that order.

Having seen what *politicians* do, we can move on to *political parties*, collections of politicians who band together to increase their chances of getting into power. There are three party games in this section. The first game is about elections, the second is about forming a government, and the third is about the interaction of these two processes. All of these games share one rather cynical assumption, which is that politicians and political parties will say anything and do anything to get into power, provided that any loss of credibility arising when they are discovered to be insincere does not outweigh the profit which such insincerity can yield. This view of politics may appeal to quite a lot of people. Others may think that it applies to most politicians and parties, but not to the ones they support. Some may think of politicians as idealists who participate in politics only to enact certain deeply held convictions, and who would not compromise these convictions one little bit in order to get into power. Such politicians may even exist, but this game is about the rest. Anyone who believes that all politicians are uncompromising idealists will already have torn this book up and thrown it away.

Politicians fight elections by making us promises. We support them if we like the promises they make, and if we believe that these promises will be carried out. In real politics, politicians make promises about all sorts of things, ranging from economic affairs (prices, wages, inflation and so on), to constitutional affairs (devolution, electoral reform and so on), to moral affairs (divorce, abortion, capital punishment and so on), to foreign affairs (treaties, foreign interventions or the lack of them). The game, however, uses only one dimension of policy, representing the social and economic decisions which underlie many of the contentious issues in modern politics. Elections consist of a struggle between parties (the players) to put forward the policy which appeals to the largest numbers of voters. Each time a party changes its policy it loses some support as the wiser electors stop believing it.

The next game is about coalitions. The object is to squeeze as much as possible out of prospective coalition partners, although if a player tries to squeeze too much he or she will be dumped by the others. Parties have to agree both on distributing the spoils and on a common policy. Even if the spoils look juicy, coalition policy may be so far from your own that you end up losing at the next election as your disillusioned supporters look elsewhere. The coalition game can be played as a sequel to the election game. This is, of course, what happens in real life. When an election will result in a coalition, the whole basis of party competition is changed. The policies which a party puts forward must not only appeal to voters, they must make the party an attractive coalition partner. Each change in policy has costs and benefits. It might increase your attractiveness to voters but reduce your chances of getting into power, or do quite the reverse.

In the final section things get really dirty. Having played politics, politicians, political parties, elections and governments, we are left with the problem of taking decisions. When small groups of self-seeking players have to agree on something, and every player knows what each of the others wants, saying what you think and doing what seems natural is a sure way to lose. If you behave like this the others can usually outsmart you by taking your likely actions into account when they make their moves. These games are therefore about sophisticated politics, in which you must take account of what the others are going to do, take account of the fact that they are taking account of what you are likely to do, and so on.

In the first of these two games, players are confronted with a series of proposals, none of which is likely to get through if only those who are really in favour support them. To get any proposal through you must recruit the support of other players who don't like what you are doing. To do this, you've got to offer them something in return, pledging your support on something which you don't like, but which your partner values very highly. This process of log-rolling can produce some very peculiar results and creates a game which is really rather complex. But then, so is politics.

The second sophisticated game is about getting your own way in a committee. The committee, which might well be a cabinet, has to take a decision on a set of issues. On each issue there are a number of possible courses of action, none of which is supported by a majority of members. You know what you want, and must try and work out what the others want, although they are hardly going to tell you straight out. Once you've done this you can set about trying to *get* what you want, using the many techniques available to sophisticated committee members. The order in which the alternatives come up for discussion, the various procedural rules, and any amount of wheeling and dealing can all work wonders for your cause. But since your opponents are trying to do the same thing to you, these calculations can get very fancy.

All kinds of deals between players are allowed in all of the games. However, as the trusting will discover to their chagrin, no deals are enforceable unless a majority of the players agrees to change the rules. The way to win most of the games (and of course the way to win at real politics) is to arrange the deals which you make so that, while each is positively to your advantage, they are all sufficiently attractive to the others to entice them into cooperating with you. You will no doubt decide to honour some of the deals you make, even when you don't have to, and even when they turn out to be to your disadvantage, so that people will believe what you say in the future. No one can win any of the games consistently without making deals, but each game has only one winner, so that your opponents will know that you are setting them up for the big one. People who want to win must learn to spot the big one coming. In trying to avoid it you will learn a lot about your friends; in trying to pull it off you will lose a lot of them. This, at least, is realistic.

WHAT YOU NEED TO PLAY POLITICS

Firstly you need some players. Ideally these should all be enemies, since this makes winning more fun. It also means that you have less to lose, since some of the players will end up hating each other. If you cannot assemble a group of enemies, a group of friends will have to do. Alternatively, you may be lucky enough to have a captive audience. You'll have to make sure they're interested, but if they are, you'll have the fun of watching them discover enemies they never realized they had, and maybe even making a few friends. The number of players is pretty flexible. Some of the games need only two players, some need five, but the upper limit is simply as large as is consistent with maintaining the most rudimentary law and order. The games change dramatically in character with different numbers of players, but this itself is interesting. 'Primitive Politics' can be played by any number of players at all, while the others are probably at their best for between three and thirty. When there are more than six players, they are usually formed into teams.

The next thing you will need is some money. A number of the games are played against Nature or a Bank, each of which is richly endowed with resources. When the games are played for real money, unless you are feeling extraordinarily philanthropic, you will have to finance the Bank by collecting an equal amount of money from each player. An amount double that which the player receives from the Bank at the start of the game is about right. The Bank can never run out of money, so if it should run into cash-flow problems as a result of the spectacular success of one or two players, a further levy will fall due from all players to finance this. Any money left in the Bank at the end of the game should be kept by whoever is organizing it. (If the other players notice this, it should be redistributed in equal shares.)

Some people, of course, don't have any money, while others don't like playing games with what they've got; in these cases you will have to improvise. Two things are needed to replace the genuine article: fake money and motivation. Fake money is the easy part. You can design your own bank notes and reproduce them on a duplicator, embezzle some from a board game (or buy it in a specialist games shop), buy counters or chips, or collect matchsticks or bottle-tops. The payoffs in these games are denominated in pounds, and you will need to produce equivalents for a fair number of £1, £5 and £10 notes. (The precise amount you will need depends on the number of players – £200 per person should suffice.) Impoverished gamblers could of course scale down the stakes and play for pennies, which do make quite effective counters. This leaves the problem of motivation, solved at a stroke if the games are played for hard currency. Even players without an inbuilt will to win often get quite involved in this type of game. Failing this the other solution is to set up a system of forfeits for the losers and rewards for the winners. As far as I know Strip Coalitions has not yet been played, but that is no reason not to try.

Apart from people and money you will need two ordinary packs of playing cards, which are doctored as appropriate for some of the games, a watch and a blackboard or large sheet of paper. Five of the seven games can be played with this basic equipment. For the two election games the only other thing you will need is a copy of the simple board which is illustrated in the text, and some counters. To make things run more smoothly you might also want to provide some simple paper badges with which the players can identify themselves, and a pocket calculator if you find simple arithmetic too painful. Having assembled the equipment, you are almost ready to play. Before describing the games in detail, however, it is worth saying a little about how best to organize things.

Each of the games has its own rules, of course, but there is provision in every game for the players to change the rules if they so desire. To stop things getting completely out of hand, however, there is a set of hard-and-fast rules, which cannot be changed, and which applies to each of the games. These rules are contained in the first chapter, and mainly consist of statements that you cannot rob the Bank, extort money from other players, and so on. For a really wild session, you might want to suspend these rules too but, if you are going to do this, you might as well throw the book away and have as much fun as you want, regardless.

One of the main points of these games is that the players should be left to discover most of the various tricks involved for themselves. Therefore, the first time that each game is played, it is just as well if people do not have too much idea of what is supposed to be going on. Each of the games is discussed in three separate sections to emphasize this point. The first section of each chapter simply gives the rules of the game and a very general description of what is going on. This section should provide enough information to play the game. It is a good idea to start playing straight away, without reading any further. The players may not know precisely what they are doing, but finding out what they should be doing is what it's all about. After one session on this basis, you may want to consult the 'how to win' section which follows. This describes some of the main strategies which should have emerged. At least, each section describes the strategies which it was intended would emerge when the games were designed! Every group of people is different, and each will impose its own character on the games, devising new strategies and tricks, and ignoring the ones which were intended. Since most of the games have provision for modifying the rules, it is impossible to predict all of the variations which might be introduced, especially since an apparently innocuous modification may have very far-reaching consequences. I hope that such modifications *are* introduced, since their consequences can be most interesting.

Without giving too much away at this stage, one example should illustrate this point. In some of the games participants often get fed up with players who continually disrupt the proceedings by proposing ridiculous deals which they never intend to comply with.

If a rule is agreed whereby all deals can be enforced then the character of each of the games is completely altered. Enforceable deals are quite different from gentlemen's agreements, particularly when gentlemen are in short supply. Alternatively, if negotiations become too protracted, people may decide to impose a time limit. They will quickly discover that this is not 'just' a time limit, however, as the character of the negotiations changes dramatically with the approach of zero hour. Thus, as well as discussing the types of strategy which should emerge, each 'how to win' section discusses the implications of some of the more obvious modifications. At this stage, it is worth playing the game again. Once the players are initiated into its mysteries, the game will probably be quite different. People can now experiment freely with alternative strategies and modifications to the rules, if this has not already happened.

The final section of each chapter discusses the relationship between the game and the real world. Much of this discussion is quite speculative, and many people will disagree with a lot of what is said. However, while the games themselves are relatively abstract, they *are* intended to relate to real politics. An obvious danger of this whole approach is that it can convey the impression that I am arguing that the real world is as simple as these games. This is obviously not the case. Each game only sets out to capture a tiny fraction of actual politics, and that very simplistically. I hope, however, that the processes discussed are interesting and that, by ruthlessly simplifying them into games, they are not trivialized. The political world is of course a rich and complicated place. The approach used in this book is to distil little bits of it and to present these in a form which sets people thinking by forcing them to participate.

1   The Fundamental Laws of Nature

The Fundamental Laws of Nature contained in this chapter apply to all of the games, and cannot be modified under any circumstances. Any player breaking any of these laws shall suffer the penalties described in Law 10. (These laws can also be applied to any other game you enjoy playing, the rules of which can then be regarded as susceptible to change if a majority of the players so desires.)

LAW 1 All rules in force at any particular time must be obeyed.

LAW 2 All dealings with Nature or the Bank must be scrupulously honest.

LAW 3 No player may attack or steal money from another player.

LAW 4 No rule may be introduced involving a further unconditional distribution of resources from Nature or the Bank to any of the players.

LAW 5 No additional rule may be introduced *enforcing* a direct payment from one player to another.

LAW 6 A player unable to meet financial commitments at any point must withdraw from the game, and cannot re-enter it in the same session.

LAW 7 Before any game is commenced, a time limit should be agreed by the players. The winner of each game is the player with the largest amount of money at the end of the specified time limit, or the only player left in the game if all other players are forced to withdraw. Once the time limit is fixed for a particular session, it cannot be altered.

LAW 8 Any of the rules of the games may be changed by an absolute majority of the players, or by a number of players previously agreed by an absolute majority.

LAW 9 Unless specifically prohibited by a rule, any form of negotiation and side payment between players is allowed.

LAW 10 Any player breaking one of these laws shall be immediately expelled from the game, forfeiting all monies held. Any further penalty that is agreed by a majority of the players shall also be enforced.

2   Primitive Politics

A game for 2–2,000,000,000 players of all ages. It should take from
1 to 1½ hours.

Primitive Politics is rather like Poker without the cards, except that
it is played against Nature as well as the other players. Although it
is easy to describe, having very few rules, it can be one of the most
complex of all of the games to play. It is also potentially the nastiest
in this book. In each round Nature supplies some of her fruits, but
only one player will receive the benefits of her generosity. The
game decides who gets what, and there is only one winner.

THE RULES

1. Each player is endowed, at the start of the game, with identical
   resources, denominated in hard cash. This amount can be varied
   by agreement between the players. A reasonable starting point
   is to provide each with £100. (Reducing this produces shorter,
   riskier, more urgent games.)
2. Nature starts the game with an additional large supply of resources, and one of the players is selected to look after her
   interests. Ideally this player should *only* do this but, since this
   involves missing out on most of the action, he or she should
   probably be allowed to play in the normal way as well.
3. Play proceeds as follows:
   (a) Each player must expend some resources in each round to
       stay alive. At the start of each round, each player contributes
       the same amount (£10 at the start of the game) to Nature
       and these funds are placed in a central kitty.
   (b) Nature matches these resources pound for pound, placing an
       amount equal to the total contributed in the central kitty.
   (c) Players then proceed to bid for the central kitty. Any player

can bid any amount, however large or small, but must place the amount of each bid in front of him or her on the table. If they wish to raise a previous bid they must place the additional cash, corresponding to the increased bid, on the table.

(d) The entire amount in the kitty is paid out to the player making the highest bid.

(e) All bids are forfeit, and returned to Nature.

(f) Any deals and side-payments between players are allowed.

(g) No deal is enforceable.

(h) Bids can only be made by individual players, and the kitty may only be paid out to an individual player.

(i) No bid may be withdrawn once made.

(j) At the end of each round, once the payout has been made, play recommences at 3(a).

HOW TO WIN PRIMITIVE POLITICS

It should very quickly become clear that some form of cooperation between the players is necessary if they are not all going to make a loss all of the time. Very superficially, it might seem that there is an obvious point at which the bidding should stop. This is when the highest bid has reached the value of the kitty, but this will prove to be a snare and a delusion. Bids already on the table are water under the bridge. This is *not* an auction, and *all* bids are forfeit. Once you have got involved in bidding, you must simply decide whether *further* bids are potentially profitable, and must write off the cost of bids already made. Say the kitty is £100 and you bid £80. Someone else bids £90. You have already lost your £80, so the real cost to you of bidding £100 for the £100 kitty is £20. If you win with this bid you have done quite well. Before you make it you stand to lose £90 on the whole game, your £10 stake and your £80 bid. If you bid £100 and win, you only lose your £10 stake. The problem is, of course, that your opponents may still try and outbid you. Put yourself in their shoes. If they don't bid again, they lose the value of their highest bid, plus the £10 stake; a winning bid of £110, on the other hand, would mean losing 'only' £20.

In fact there is no 'natural' point at which the bidding should stop. If the bids are units of £10 and there are two people in the bidding, for example, then every new bid makes a *potential* net profit of £80 when the prize is a £100 kitty. The same is still true if the bids reach a million pounds! Two players caught up in bidding against each other are committed to a diabolical sequence of bid and counterbid which can only end in mutual ruin.

One alternative, taking this into account, is not to bid at all. This is hardly an inspiring strategy, since it represents a gradual decline into genteel poverty at the rate of £10 per game. The only way you will win if you do this is if everyone else goes crazy, bidding each other into the ground at a faster rate than your gradual decline.

Despite all of this, there is obviously money to be made in this game. Since Nature is matching the original stake money pound for pound, the group's stock of resources is *potentially* increasing. One way to tap this source of revenue is for all of the players to co-operate. If they all get together and agree that one of them shall bid £1 for the kitty, subsequently dividing the profits between them, they can all make a profit. If there are five players, the kitty will be £100 (£50 in stake money and £50 from Nature). If all five get together, bid £1 and then share the kitty out at £20 each, each will make a net profit on the round of £10. Not surprisingly, this is not as simple as it seems at first sight.

Firstly, since there is only one ultimate winner, someone will have to break ranks and try to double-cross the others. If all of the players decide that they will share the prize between them, every one of them has an incentive to back out of the deal. Imagine that five players have got together and agreed to split the kitty. They nominate one of their number to make the bid. As soon as this is done, one of the others breaks ranks and makes a counter-bid, reminding the rest of what happens if they all start up a cycle of competitive bidding. The renegade might even promise never to do it again. Since no deals are binding, there is nothing to stop anyone doing this. The rest of the group is now faced with an interesting set of problems. They can capitulate, and let the wildcat bidder take the kitty. This person will then make a handsome profit, for a slightly larger investment taking the whole kitty instead of just one fifth of it. Alternatively the others could force the wildcat out of the game, since between them they command more resources than any individual does. They could use these to bid regardless, making a loss on this one round, but bankrupting the wildcat and removing a threat to their profit in the long term. Finally, they could try threatening a firm response, hoping that they can force the wildcat back into line. Thus the consortium bids, he bids against them, reminding them of the dangers of escalation, and they bid against him, announcing their intention to bankrupt him if he does not rejoin the group. This is the first of a long line of threats and promises which might now ensue. The wildcat may drop out when confronted with this threat from his former colleagues, but he can go one stage further and counter with a threat *and* a promise. He can say that he intends to fight this one out to the bitter end, forcing the others to force him out, at considerable cost to them, but coupling this threat with a promise that he will rejoin them *next* round. The group must now decide whether to believe him. If they do they should decide not to carry out the threat they have made, back down, and hope to reap the future benefits of long-term cooperation without incurring the cost of punishing the wildcat. If they don't believe him, they should force him out anyway, since this is best done sooner rather than later.

Whatever the outcome, this episode will result in a rethinking of the deal to exploit Nature. Players will want to look for agreements which are somehow proof against being exploited by a wildcat. There are two basic types of agreement which might achieve this. Both are conditional. The first is to build the threat to retaliate against defectors into the deal, which would now look like this: 'We will agree to cooperate, making only one bid and equally dividing the spoils which we extract from Nature. If anyone breaks this agreement, we will force them out of the game, using our superior combined resources.' This agreement, by making a specific threat to punish the wildcats, may deter people from trying it on. The alternative is to make a more general threat along the following lines: 'We agree to cooperate, making only one bid and equally dividing the spoils which we extract from Nature. If anyone breaks this agreement, it is automatically rendered void.' In other words if we all cooperate, fine, but if anyone breaks ranks it's back to the jungle. This might deter wildcats, although some may still decide to try and take the money and run, hoping to weather the subsequent storm. This deal will also tend to break down as the game draws to a close, since the storms to be weathered will get shorter and shorter. The smaller the number of remaining games, the more attractive it will be to make a quick killing and then keep your head down.

In fact, if there is a finite and known number of games things will always be more unstable. Obviously all hell will break loose in the final game, since no punishments can be carried out in subsequent rounds. Since all hell is bound to break loose in the ultimate game, all hell should also break loose in the penultimate game, for the same reasons. And so on.

We have seen that agreements that are not binding can be very unstable. In addition, there is no guarantee that the member of the group who actually makes the bid and receives the payoff will go on to share the winnings with the others, despite being threatened with the same sanctions as a wildcat bidder. It will quickly emerge, if these informal agreements do not work, that some means of making *binding* agreements is necessary. This needs a change in the rules, which can be achieved by an absolute majority of the members. Such a change might make binding all agreements which are somehow ratified, with specific penalties for defection. The method of deciding when an agreement has been ratified and the nature of the penalties to be enacted will have to be specified, and this will be a matter for negotiation between the players. For example, agreements which are written down may be binding on those who initial them, or verbal agreements cemented by a handshake or witnessed by Nature may be held inviolable. Obviously, the more determined and wily potential wildcats are, the more carefully these arrangements must be considered. Penalties can include exclusion from the game, cash fines or any other punishment or humiliation the group finds appropriate.

Introducing binding agreements is only one of the many rule-changes which should be considered. Another obvious candidate is the rule which specifies the majority needed to change a rule. One possible development which can emerge is exploitation of one group of players by another, larger group. The agreement to cooperate and exploit the fruits of Nature need not be made between *all* of the players. A majority could get together and agree to do this, threatening the others with annihilation if they do not acquiesce. The others may decide not to comply if they face a slow decline into oblivion, but the majority group could agree to take the whole kitty, paying the outsiders back their stake money each round so that they can maintain themselves at a bare subsistence level. This would greatly increase the well-being of the majority at the expense of the minority, since only the majority would share the extra resources contributed by Nature, instead of dividing this between all of the players. Members of the majority who become scared of being left out in the cold may, however, be prepared to support rule-changes which increase the size of the majority needed to change any rule, thereby providing some protection against exploitation. Members of this majority may be quite justified in these fears, since the players left out of the agreement may be prepared to offer attractive terms to the others to be let in. The poorest members of the majority will therefore feel threatened by individuals in the minority, since the latter will presumably be prepared to take anything more than they are getting to be allowed into the majority.

This brief discussion obviously only scratches the surface of all of the strategic possibilities of Primitive Politics. There are many other ways of winning, and the number of innovations which can be introduced is almost endless. To go further into them in an abstract way would be rather boring since many of the points which could be made will only relate to particular groups with particular styles and nasty habits. The game is obviously completely different when played by a trusting group than when played by a suspicious one. It is also completely different when played by a large group than by a small one. The larger the group, the less likely it is that conditional agreements will succeed, and the more likely that a system of binding agreements will emerge, and so on. Rather than getting involved in all of this, the best thing for me to do is to get back to reality.

REALITY

You will already have seen that there is a lot of politics in this game. It sets out to explore the ways in which a group of people organize their lives and take advantage of the benefits they can realize from cooperating, when stabbing each other in the back appears a superficially more attractive prospect. Most of all, of course, each member of the group would like to let the *others* cooperate while he or she reaps the benefits without contributing. This is one of the fundamental problems of politics, if not *the* fundamental problem. The game starts off with no formal institutions and no formal arrangements to encourage people towards this sort of cooperation. As the game develops, these institutions and arrangements tend to emerge.

In the most general terms, the game sets the players the problem of coexisting without politics, a problem referred to by some political theorists as a 'state of nature' problem. Rather more precisely, it is the problem of how to produce public goods, which are goods which everyone in a particular group or society can enjoy, whether or not they contribute towards the costs of providing them. Providing public goods is one of the main functions of the most modern political systems, and examples of public goods include national security, internal security, clean air, public health services, road systems and so on. Thus, while everyone would agree that some organization designed to put out fires is in the public interest, if firemen went around with collecting boxes asking for voluntary contributions towards the costs of the fire service, they would probably not get enough to buy the new fire-engines, breathing apparatus and turntable ladders they need to do their job effectively. Governments step into the breach by forcing us 'for our own good' to contribute towards the costs of providing these services. A major part of political debate concerns deciding precisely *which* services are public goods, to be provided by governments, and precisely *how* they should be provided.

In the game, an agreement between the players to cooperate is a public good. It enables everyone to do better than if they all come into continual conflict with each other. The stability brought about by such an agreement can be enjoyed by everyone, whether or not they are party to it. Indeed, it can be enjoyed *more* by the non-cooperators, since they can take advantage of the others. There is no government in the game. One of the purposes of the game is to explore the arguments for and against a government which would regulate the players and punish the wildcats. The other main purpose of the game is to show that, even without a government, some forms of cooperation can emerge which solve the problem. Indeed, to win at all, people are forced into such cooperation. They must try and organize themselves socially without a government. The players are forced, therefore, to be anarchists.

'Anarchist' solutions to social problems are not, in these terms, nearly as exotic as they might sound; we participate in them every day in modern society. There is no law which compels people waiting for a bus to stand in an orderly line. A wildcat who joins a long queue at the front cannot be disqualified from the game by being imprisoned, deported or executed, attractive as these alternatives might seem to those waiting behind. If there are large or heavily armed people standing at the back of the queue, the sinner might be persuaded to step into line. Whatever happens, however, he or she will almost certainly live to queue again, despite having broken the unwritten social agreement about how to wait for buses.

The bus queue is a good example of the sort of conditional agreement we discussed in the previous section. Not only is it completely unenforceable by anything other than physical or verbal violence, which is generally ruled out by the absolute rules of the game, but it tends to collapse very quickly when confronted with defectors. Watching a rapidly filling bus with only a few seats left and a few people surging forward to get those seats, you can often witness the purest chaos. Examples of this type of informal social anarchy are legion. Anyone who has been to an open-air concert will know that things are much better if everyone sits down. If a few people stand up, then other people whose view is blocked also stand up. Soon everyone is standing up and still seeing less. All get tired and grumpy, and nearly everyone is worse off. Sitting down at open-air concerts is a public good produced by informal agreement which is, unfortunately, not very stable. A public park is a joy to behold if it is unsullied by empty crisp packets and banana skins. As long as it is clean, people tend to want to keep it clean, and are less likely to throw their rubbish all around them. Once a few have thrown their rubbish around, however, it looks less nice and matters less if it is littered. So it gets littered more and more and ends up looking like a rubbish dump.

Many other facets of social and political life are governed by unenforceable collective agreements, explicit or tacit. Two obvious areas where these are particularly important are the criminal underworld (which obviously cannot use the powers of government to regulate itself, yet manages to preserve some form of orderly organization) and international politics (where no world government can force national governments to do something they don't want to do). In each case, order is maintained, and the appropriate public goods produced, by the same mix of agreement, threat and promise which characterizes the game of Primitive Politics. At a national level, an important example is provided by the behaviour of trade unions facing a possible wages explosion. Even when government enforcement is out of the question, if union leaders realize that a wages explosion would be collectively damaging, they can agree to restrain their demands as long as everyone else does too. A conditional agreement emerges to produce the perceived public good of wage restraint which operates only as long as no one breaks ranks. The stability which is produced is rather fragile. Everyone watches everyone else, and as soon as one union breaks through the policy the deal quickly collapses. Most of all, we would like everyone else to take part in wage restraint, but to let us burst right through it.

The other thing which the game sets out to demonstrate is the importance of some mechanism for making agreements binding. Such a mechanism is one of the most fundamental of all public goods, advocated even by most of those who want only the most minimal level of government intervention. A system of binding agreements greatly increases the chance that public goods will be produced, since otherwise people cannot be sure that the deals they make with each other will be carried out. In real politics it is of course ultimately the government, through the legal system, which enforces most agreements. The interesting thing is that, in those areas of our lives which are not suited to government intervention, there is nearly always some alternative system available to enable us to make binding agreements with each other and hence to increase our production of public goods. Returning once more to the underworld, the power of organized crime syndicates is based upon the fact that it is unwise to double-cross The Man. Agreements made with a syndicate have a way of getting enforced. In its own terms the syndicate is quite right to take a considerable loss ensuring that any particular agreement is enforced, so that potential double-crossers know what to expect. A concrete overcoat may be an expensive way to punish a small-time chiseller, but it's cheap at ten times the price if it keeps everybody else in line.

Similarly, there are many financial transactions undertaken by ordinary folk where the sums involved are too great to really feel happy about trusting the other party. The state's system of enforcing contracts might not be much good if the profits from a single double-cross are sufficiently large to make it worth taking the money and running for the safety of a system where its jurisdiction does not apply. In these cases transactions are effected by using intermediaries who are locked into and bound by some system of enforcing agreements. These include banks, who are subject to effective government enforcement, solicitors, who regulate themselves via national organizations like the Law Society, and so on. Indeed almost any group of people who wish to establish sufficient credibility to make important deals attempts to set up some form of regulatory body which includes among its duties the enforcement of agreements made by its members.

Primitive Politics illustrates a theme which will recur throughout the rest of this book, that much of politics is concerned with providing means to reconcile the mixed motives of conflict and cooperation which characterize our social life. While many people are concerned to further their own personal well-being, they are aware that this can only be achieved by sacrificing short-term personal considerations in favour of longer-term social cooperation. Even the most selfish individuals must do this, despite the fact that they are solely concerned to maximize their own welfare. One function of political institutions is to regulate the behaviour produced by this contradictory set of motivations. Yet, even in those social situations where institutions do not or cannot operate, more informal types of political interaction can develop to fulfil the same purpose.

3 Entrepreneurs

A game for three to thirty players of all ages. It should take from $1\frac{1}{2}$ to 2 hours.

One way of solving some of the problems highlighted by the previous game is for someone to coordinate our activities and supply the public goods which we find it so difficult to produce on our own. If our system contains only one such person with a deeply entrenched position we will not be much better off, since this monopoly position will probably lead to very few public goods being produced. Someone who would be concerned solely to grow rich at our expense, and who has no serious challengers, will not have to perform very well. Being such a leader is potentially a very profitable position; one way of avoiding abuse of this situation is to make sure that the leader is kept up to scratch by the threat of competition. If there are other people who would like to be in power, the leader is forced to concentrate on performing well, for fear of losing that meal-ticket. Entrepreneurs is about this type of competition, for the coveted position of leader of the pack.

THE RULES

1. In each round of the game two of the players compete with each other to be selected by the remaining players as leader. Once selected, the leader must produce a budget based on the players' preferences on four important areas of expenditure. These areas of expenditure are:
   (a) Defence
   (b) Welfare
   (c) Industry
   (d) Public works
2. In the first round one of the players is selected to be the incum-

bent leader, by drawing straws, cutting cards, or whatever. The
player on his or her immediate right is the first challenger. If
more than ten players are playing, then the incumbent and the
challenger are represented by teams of two players, if more than
twenty are playing, by teams of three players. The remaining
players always play as individuals, except when they form part
of a challenging or incumbent team.

3. Each player receives £100 at the start of the game. One player is
selected to represent the interests of Nature.

4. Each round of play proceeds as follows :

(a) Every player except the incumbent and the challenger must
first decide upon how they would like the £100 budget to be
spent. There are four policies available for expenditure. Each
player writes down *in secret* his or her preferred expenditure
on each of these policies, bearing in mind that total expenditure must not exceed £100. (There is no advantage in allo-
cating *less* than £100.) This is the only restriction on the way
in which players can allocate their preferences. These can be
distributed evenly between all policies, completely devoted
to any one policy, or anything else between these extremes.
Players may start off by listing the expenditure they would
actually like to see incurred on the various issues. Later in
the game tactical considerations will undoubtedly outweigh
personal preference.

(b) Each player writes his or her name on the statement of
preferred policy, folds the paper in half, and hands it to
Nature for safe keeping. These pieces of paper must not be
looked at again until the elected leader has declared his or
her policies.

(c) A five-minute period of negotiation now takes place. During
this time any player may talk to any other, in public or in
private. The players will probably want to lobby both the
incumbent and the challenger, revealing as much or as little
about their actual preferences as they see fit, in an attempt to
influence the character of the policies which each will put
forward.

(d) At the end of five minutes, all negotiation must stop. The incumbent and challenger are now able to decide upon the policy which they will enact if elected to office. They must write this policy on a piece of paper, specifying the amount that they intend to spend on each of the four areas of national security, health and welfare, industry and public works. *Total expenditure must equal* £100. These policies are handed to Nature for safe keeping, and no player is allowed to look at them.

(e) The election campaign now starts. The incumbent and the challenger each make a two-minute speech which reveals as much or as little as they choose about the policies that they intend to enact. These speeches need bear no relation at all to what they actually intend to do after being elected. The incumbent decides upon the order of speaking.

(f) Following the speeches, there is a five-minute question-and-answer session during which any player is able to ask any question of either candidate. (Unruly groups may wish to select someone to chair this session.)

(g) Following the question-and-answer session the election is held by *secret ballot*. Each player writes the name of their favoured candidate on a piece of paper, and these ballot papers are handed to Nature. After the voting has finished, the papers are shuffled and then counted. The candidate with the most votes is declared the winner.

(h) Now that a winner has been declared, each player must pay taxes. Each, including the losing candidate, must pay £50 to the winner of the election. In addition, Nature pays the leader £40 for every player in the game.

(i) The moment of truth has now arrived. The policy of the winner is revealed. *The policy of the losing candidate must be destroyed*, and under no circumstances can it be revealed.

(j) These policies are put into practice, and benefit the players as follows:

– if the actual policy enacted on an issue involves *more expenditure than that preferred* by the player on the issue, the leader pays the player the value the player would have preferred to see enacted;

— if the actual policy enacted on an issue is *equal to or less than that preferred* by the player, the leader pays the player the value of the policy enacted.

In other words, for each policy issue, the leader pays each player either the value the player would have preferred, or the value enacted by the leader, whichever is the less.

(k) Once the payouts have been made, preparations start for the next election. The next player, or team, to the right of the previous challenger takes up the challenge. Play recommences at 4(a).

5. Play continues until every player has contested an election. When this stage has been reached, the players may, by majority vote, decide to have another complete round, in which every player will contest at least one further election.

HOW TO WIN ENTREPRENEURS

Strategies for playing this game, of course, vary depending on whether you are a mere mortal or one of the two aspiring leaders. Since there is almost no point of similarity between the two roles, the respective strategies will be handled in separate sections.

Leadership strategies

Aspiring leaders are torn between the desire to get elected and the desire to make a profit when they have done so. To get elected, a candidate must obviously please as many voters as possible. This is achieved by producing policies which are as close as possible to those of a majority of voters, or at least by claiming that the policies are close to the ones which people want. A winning candidate must not only produce attractive policies but also be believed by the others. Yet if the policies directly correspond to those of a large number of players, the winner of the election will make a loss. Your alleged policies must be close enough to win the election and make friends, but not so close that you lose money.

The players may at first choose their preferred policies at random. In this case it is very unlikely that the winner will make a loss, since it will be extremely unlikely that all of the players will have similar preferences. Therefore it will be very unlikely that the leader will be faced with having to make a maximum payout. After a while, however, the preferred policies of the players should start to converge (see below). Once this has happened, there may be a large group of players, each of whom has a similar set of policy preferences. In these cases, as challenger or as incumbent you'll want to make your alleged policies close enough to win support, and hence the election, but not so close that you make a loss if you get elected. In the short term you can lie about your policies when you make your speeches. If you do this too blatantly, however, the others will stop believing you and probably stop voting for you. You want to make a profit. You can only make a profit if you are elected. To get elected you must be as straightforward as possible. If you are too straightforward you will make a loss.

One way out of this dilemma is to be *vague* about your policies. You will need to say enough to give the impression that these policies will be popular with a majority of the players. You want them to vote for you, but you must not say so much that your supporters will be able either to leave you with no profit or to detect every little lie you tell them to increase your payment. How vague you can be will depend upon how your opponent decides to play things. Faced with a very explicit opponent, proposing detailed and popular policies, you will be forced to be rather specific, otherwise the voters will get suspicious. Your opponent may be so specific and so popular that he or she is bound to get elected, but also will be bound to make a loss. This means that it is almost always better to make your speech after your opponent (and you can exercise this built-in advantage if you are the incumbent). That way you can take your opponent's strategy into account when you make your own appeal to the voters.

After the first election has taken place the record of the incumbent will become a campaign issue in itself. An incumbent who is straightforward and truthful will develop an advantage over a charlatan in the eyes of the other players. Honesty may lose money in the short term but may pay dividends in the longer term if it results in continual re-election. Your opponents will always try to exploit every discrepancy between your promises and your record in office. The fewer of these discrepancies there are, the less ammunition they will have. As we have seen, inconsistencies between what you say and what you do can be reduced either by telling the whole truth or by telling very little. However, for continued re-election, there is no substitute for a happy electorate, provided that they are not so happy that you make a loss.

When you are deciding on the policy which you will put forward, what you actually propose will depend on how much you know about the policies of the voters. The more you know, the easier this becomes. Voters may reveal quite a lot to you, or they may reveal very little. They may tell the truth or they may lie. You will have to use your skill and knowledge of them to extract as much information from them as you can to work out what to believe. Obviously, the more straightforward *you* are, the more straightforward *they* are likely to be with you. Once you have double-crossed your electorate, they may stop telling you the truth, trying to double-cross you in return and increase their profits. While *you* have the opportunity to cheat the *voters*, *they* have the opportunity to cheat *you*, and you should bear this in mind in all your calculations. If you know everything about their preferences, you simply have to decide how straightforward to be. If you know little about their preferences, then you will have to decide how risky a strategy you want to play. You could put all your eggs in one basket by placing all of your expenditure under one heading, hoping to sweep the board. In this case you will have to be careful what you say if you want to retain any credibility at all. Alternatively, you could distribute expenditure more evenly across the various policies, leaving you more things to (honestly) tell more people while reducing your potential profits.

Another important problem to consider is the possibility of collusion, either with voters or with the other candidate. Having friends in the voting population is an advantage for any candidate. One or more voters can be encouraged to ask your opponent awkward questions, or persuaded not to ask you awkward questions. They can act as a catalyst for agreements between voters which help you make a profit and generally behave as *agents provocateurs*. They can be rewarded by you for these services either by a straight fee or, if this is felt to be indelicate, with some inside information about your intended policies which will enable them to make a profitable choice of policies for themselves. (This is effectively a covert payment from you to them.) This of course exposes you to the risk that the information you disclose will be relayed to others and put to profitable use by them. It has the advantage that, if you are not double-crossed, your collusion may be undetected.

Collusion with the other candidate can also be very profitable. You could, for example, both agree to propose very similar policies and split the profits when one of you is elected. While this may yield very lucrative returns in a single election, you must remember that such an agreement is easy to detect. You must face a new challenger at the next election, and if you cannot corrupt him or her in the same way, you will face almost certain defeat. The knowledge that you face almost certain defeat will furthermore make subsequent challengers rather difficult to corrupt, since in confronting you with this, they will be able to present the voters with an attractive position representing a very powerful combination of virtue and self-interest.

All of the leadership strategies we have discussed boil down to balancing on the one hand the short-term attraction of cheating the voters, taking the money and running, and on the other hand the long-term attractions of honesty, producing continual (but less profitable) re-election. In the first instance you are as cynical and devious as you can be, giving up any attempt to maintain appearances. In the second instance you are as cynical and devious as you can be, giving up short-term profits to maintain a vestige of credibility.

Voter strategies

Voters have much less freedom of action than the candidates. However, they do have important decisions to take, and must try and make a profit out of each round. The important activity occurs at three stages in the game, when you decide on your preferred policy, when you lobby the candidates, and when you cast your vote.

The first is perhaps the least obvious. Naïve voters may regard their choice of preferred policy as largely arbitrary. They will soon discover that it is not. As I mentioned above, if the voters all decide their policies independently, they cannot possibly make as much profit as they would if they got together and coordinated this process. All voters will not want to collude, since this helps them all equally, and there is only one winner. The ideal size for a group of colluding voters is sufficiently large to influence one or other of the candidates, but not so large that the candidates have to double-cross the group for fear of making a loss when elected. There may therefore be several groups of colluding voters, each trying to bring pressure to bear on the different candidates. The group will want to decide upon a common policy, although this agreement cannot be enforced since each voter makes his or her final selection of policy in private. Having decided upon a policy, they must decide upon how much or how little to reveal to which of the candidates. They must decide whether to tell the truth or to lie; they must decide whether to be specific or vague in the information they reveal. They may decide to appoint a representative to conduct all negotiations with the candidates in order to reduce the risk of telling the candidates different stories. If they do appoint such a representative, however, they expose themselves to the risk that he or she will do a clandestine deal with one of the candidates, and sell them down the river (see above).

The process of bringing pressure to bear upon the candidates, whether individually or in groups, involves skills both of advocacy and of wheeling and dealing. It is probable that both candidates will be approached, and the most favourable deal extracted from one in exchange for an (unenforceable) promise to vote for them. Apart from the obvious need to persuade and convince, you will probably get involved in making threats and promises. You can, for example, threaten to support an opponent if a more attractive policy package is not promised. You can even threaten to do this if the alternative on offer is less attractive. If the candidates are colluding, of course, they will be impervious to threats of this nature, although you could then attempt to break up this collusion by offering a cast-iron majority to one in exchange for policy concessions. You will face the same problem as the candidates in trying to weigh up the relative advantages of honesty and dishonesty, explicitness and vagueness. On the one hand you may want to promise to vote for both candidates in exchange for concessions from each, ending up voting for one and double-crossing the other. If the candidate you double-cross ends up the winner, it will obviously be much harder to do a deal the next time around. Similarly, if you tell the candidate exactly what you want, you expose yourself to the risk that this information will be used against you. Despite this, you must disclose enough to enable the candidate to help you if he or she decides to do so.

When it comes to voting, your opportunities for devious behaviour are enhanced by the fact that the ballot is secret, unless this rule is changed. Thus there is some chance that a double-cross will remain undetected. This is one disadvantage of belonging to a group, since the chance that a candidate will notice non-delivery of the votes of a whole group is obviously greater than the chance of missing a single recalcitrant. In addition to cheating an individual candidate, you can also cheat any group of which you are a member, presumably after having made a private deal with one of the candidates to set the others up for a killing. This of course is easy to detect when the payoffs are made, unless a rule is passed that these sordid transactions are conducted in private. Detection will of course reduce potentially profitable cooperation in the future.

Thus the general nature of the problems faced by voters is rather similar to the nature of problems faced by candidates, although these problems manifest themselves in different ways. The main difference between voters and candidates is that candidates can make much larger profits when they succeed, although everyone gets the chance to be a candidate in turn, while voters have more opportunity both to collude and to double-cross without fear of detection.

Finally, we come to possible changes in the rules which might emerge. These include, as before, the development of some method of enforcing ratified agreements. This may appear to be attractive since the problem of broken deals is similar to that manifested in the previous game. The same can be said of any move to alter the majority needed to pass any change in the rules. The major new type of rule-change which might develop involves the disclosure of information. At the beginning of the game, everyone's real policy preference, and everyone's vote, is secret. If a large amount of double-crossing goes on, these rules might be changed; perhaps to allow people to reveal their precise preferences if they wish, perhaps to force people to reveal their preferences under certain circumstances (if they are making a ratified deal, for example), perhaps to make voting public. The reasoning behind each of these should be clear from the previous discussion. In each case disclosure of information makes deals easier to set up by restricting the possibility of undetected double-crossing. Lastly, if a particular candidate has done well by colluding, either with other candidates or with other voters, rules may be enacted to prohibit this. It is probable, however, that no rule or set of rules can be constructed which completely eliminates the possibility of any form of corruption. Which takes us back to reality.

REALITY

The previous game was played directly against Nature. In this game there are intermediaries, the candidates for election. The successful candidate collects taxes, extracts resources from nature, and redistributes these to the players, hoping to retain a significant surplus for personal satisfaction. This game therefore presents politicians as entrepreneurs, attempting to make a profit by providing public goods to the electorate in much the same way as those involved in business, who try to make a profit by providing private goods to consumers. The fact that political entrepreneurs make a profit from their activities does not necessarily mean that their 'consumers' are getting a bad deal. They value the goods the politician provides, such as national security, health programmes and so on. As we saw in the previous game, without some form of leadership it is possible that these goods will not be produced at all. By coordinating everyone's activities and producing these goods, politicians can provide real benefits to their clients, despite their profit. This is just the same as a private entrepreneur, who *may* provide you with a product you value quite highly at the price and still make a profit. It may well be better and cheaper than you could have produced on your own because the entrepreneur has access to a wider market, can use economies of scale, can specialize in doing just this one thing well, and so on.

Because the politician can make a profit from these activities, there will be competition from others who want to take over. The threat posed by competition means that politicians must pay careful attention to the desires of their clients. If they don't, somebody else will. This does not mean that they must fulfil those desires, but simply that they must be taken into account when the politician makes decisions. This means that the clients, who have their own ideas about what politicians should produce, can attempt to exploit the competition for office by bargaining their support for particular candidates in exchange for policy concessions. This is the process which this game sets out to capture.

In reality, of course, politicians do not (legally) hang on to all of the profits which they make from collecting taxes and producing public goods. Nevertheless, most politicians are motivated by a strong desire to get into power. What this game assumes is that these motives are not *entirely* philanthropic. This game, then, is about competition for the private satisfactions of office (such as power, status, a salary and so on) when the function of the office is to raise social well-being.

From the point of view of politicians, the essential dilemma portrayed by the game is the choice between straightforwardness and deviousness. Straightforward politicians will tend to be popular with the electorate. They will, like all politicians, take account of electoral preferences and attempt to win support by reconciling these as best they can. When people have different ideas about the policies which should be enacted, they obviously cannot satisfy everyone. They must attempt to produce a policy which looks better than any other to a majority of the population. The electors must, of course, take politicians on trust, but straightforward politicians will tend to honour their promises, not because they think this is the right thing to do, but because they think it is the most profitable thing to do.

The private entrepreneur would like to produce shoddy goods if at all possible, but the danger of losing to a competitor in the market limits the possibilities in this direction. It is necessary to keep up the quality of output. Politicians are in a similar position. It might always be more profitable to take the money and run in the short term, making promises which cannot, or will not, be honoured, in exchange for the profits of a single term of office. Faced with a politician who takes this view of politics, the system of competition provides no safeguards for the electorate whatsoever. But an astute politician will weigh against the short-term costs of keeping election promises the prospect of gaining the voters' confidence in the long term.

Thus the far-sighted politician tends to *appear* more straightforward than the short-sighted one. But it should also emerge from the game that there are ways and ways of being straightforward. These basically relate to the amount of information which a politician is prepared to reveal about his or her intended programme. We saw that being too explicit has a major drawback. It involves making promises which it might not be possible to fulfil profitably. Since failure to deliver is likely to be punished by the voters in the next round, promises must be made carefully. All sorts of excuses can of course be produced for failure to fulfil campaign pledges, and this element of political entrepreneurship is absent from the game. Devious players can try to make excuses, but they are not likely to impress without the International Monetary Fund, foreign speculators, trade unions, OPEC or other convenient scapegoats to fall back upon. Many issues of contemporary politics do remain within the competence of politicians, however, and the game demonstrates the logic of waffle in these matters. The less you reveal about your programme, the less obviously you can fall short of it. The bad news is that the less explicit you are, the less impressed voters will be by what you have to say. Your opponent, of course, sees things from the other side. He or she will try and force you to be explicit when this embarrasses you, or leave you standing by making an explicit statement when this appears to their advantage. The incumbent government always has to be quite explicit, since it actually has to *do* things, so its freedom of manoeuvre is always less than the opposition's. The government will therefore devote considerable energy to attempting to force the opposition to show its hand as early and as explicitly as possible. Indeed a large part of political debate concerns attempts by one band of politicians to nail down another on a particular issue of policy, together with corresponding attempts by the others to wriggle out of unequivocal commitments. Sometimes, but more rarely, the process is reversed. Once a positive electoral preference becomes clear on a particular issue, politicians can vie with each other to jump in and commit themselves before their opponents.

As far as the voters are concerned, the game demonstrates some of the logic of pressure-group activity. Voters can combine very effectively to lobby the candidates, trading their support for policy concessions. More importantly, a group which controls a large enough block of votes to be worth bothering with will be able to play off the opposing candidates against each other. If this is carried out in public, the group can attempt to set up a straightforward policy auction. If bargaining is conducted in private, then an auction with a difference can be started. The difference is that the group can lie to the candidates about what their opponents have offered. In either case, the position of the group is strengthened by the secret-ballot system, which means that it can back out of any deal it has made in the hope of not being detected. This in turn will make politicians rather unwilling to deal with pressure groups entirely on the basis of voting support. They will want something more tangible, such as financial or organizational help with their campaigns, before giving away any valuable policy concessions.

Finally, we can see that a pressure group can increase its bargaining strength by confining itself to members who have very similar policy preferences. The more consistent the group, the easier it is to deal with and the more concrete the demands it can make. Discussion of a coherent platform is an important part of pressure-group politics, although this platform does not necessarily have to be revealed in any of its public pronouncements. Pressure groups can waffle to good advantage, thereby avoiding revealing information which might make them easier to outflank. Pressure groups can also lie about their objectives, although, given the problem which we have seen to be associated with this, they have less reason to do so than politicians, since they are less obliged to stick to any deals which they make.

The overall consequence of this competition between political entrepreneurs for the spoils of office is that both politicians and voters may well end up better off. The voters pay taxes and, if they organize themselves properly, can receive more than they pay out in return. The politicians receive the taxes, as well as a hefty contribution from Nature, while supplying public goods and keeping the profits. One thing can transform this situation quite dramatically, however. This is collusion between politicians. If the opposing candidates agree between themselves not to compete on the basis of offering attractive policies, or to offer any policy which seems popular, with no intention of honouring it, then they can try to make much more money than before by organizing their actual policies so that most electors pay their taxes and get almost nothing in return. As far as the game is concerned, such collusion is relatively easy to legislate against, although such legislation will be difficult to enforce because collusion is not always easy to detect. In reality things are rather more difficult. Not only can negotiations between politicians take place in complete secrecy, but such negotiations do take place all the time, for all sorts of reasons. The political system would obviously grind to a halt if all forms of cooperation between politicians were to be banned, yet, once cooperation is taking place, it is very difficult to define some as undesirable and the rest as all right. Yet such cooperation can clearly lead to 'conspiracies of silence' in which all sides refuse to commit themselves to a position on an issue dear to the hearts of the general public, or a significant subsection of it representing, perhaps, a particular ethnic, religious, linguistic or social group.

Entrepreneurs demonstrates the pressures on self-seeking politicians when they attempt to formulate policies which are popular enough to get them elected into office while still enabling them to make a profit when they get there. To increase these pressures voters form themselves into groups, and, to respond to them, politicians can resort to lying, waffling and even to telling the truth.

4 Elections

A game for two to thirty players. It should take from 1 to 1½ hours.

Each of the players controls a political party attempting to find the policies which appeal to the broadest cross-section of the electorate. The electorate has widely differing opinions on the best policy, but each group will always vote for the party which has the policy which is closest to its own. Parties therefore compete with each other to produce the policy which commands most support, although the swings and roundabouts of the election campaign can upset these calculations.

EQUIPMENT

1. A bundle of money.
2. Twenty-one black counters (any other colour, I suppose, would do).
3. A different counter, or marker, for each party.
4. A pack of playing cards for determining the election results. All hearts must be removed before starting to play. The jokers, of course, are left in.
5. A copy of the playing board, which is reproduced here.
6. Simple badges can be made to identify the political parties.

THE RULES

Setting up the game

1. The board shows the range of possible policies for the political parties on the most important issue of the day, the level of direct taxation to be paid by the electorate. These policies are

SWING

L ← → R

VOTES

2000																			2000
1900																			1900
1800																			1800
1700																			1700
1600																			1600
1500								▨	▨	▨									1500
1400							▨					▨							1400
1300						▨						▨							1300
1200																			1200
1100					▨								▨						1100
1000																			1000
900				▨										▨					900
800																			800
700			▨												▨				700
600		▨														▨			600
500	▨																▨		500
400																		▨	400
300																			300
200																			200
100																			100

| 60% | 58% | 56% | 54% | 52% | 50% | 48% | 46% | 44% | 42% | 40% | 38% | 36% | 34% | 32% | 30% | 28% | 26% | 24% | 22% |

POLICY
(Tax rate.)

PARTY GAMES BOARD

arranged in order along the bottom of the board, and range from 60 per cent on the far left to 22 per cent on the far right.

2. Above each of these policy positions is a column on which one of the black counters is placed to represent the number of voters favouring this policy. This counter is moved up and down at each election to reflect the results.

3. At the beginning of the game electoral opinion is distributed, and the counters are positioned, as follows :

Tax Rates	No. of voters
60 per cent & 22 per cent	400
58 per cent & 24 per cent	500
56 per cent & 26 per cent	600
54 per cent & 28 per cent	700
52 per cent & 30 per cent	900
50 per cent & 32 per cent	1100
48 per cent & 34 per cent	1300
46 per cent & 36 per cent	1400
44 per cent–38 per cent	1500

(These starting positions are lightly shaded on the board.) This means that the main body of electoral opinion is clustered in the middle of the board, with high or low tax rates being less popular.

4. Each player is given £100 in campaign funds and choses a political party to represent. If there are more than six players, six teams are formed to control the parties. The six parties in the game are :
National Defence League (NDL)
People's Revolutionary Alliance (PRA)
Radical Socialists (RS)
Progressive Party (PP)
Reform Party (RP)
Freedom Party (FP)

The election campaign

5. The first round of the game is a little different, because the parties must establish their initial policies. The pack of election

cards is first shuffled and cut by each player to decide the order of play. (Aces low, jokers high, the highest player goes first.)

6. The players declare their policy on income tax in turn. They each do this by placing their marker on the policy square of their choice. No party can occupy a square which is already occupied by another party.

7. A coin is tossed to decide the direction of the swing in the *previous* election (heads it was left, tails it was right). This is recorded by placing the final black counter in the appropriate position on the swing indicator.

8. The remaining part of this campaign, and the whole of each subsequent campaign, consists of parties jostling each other for position. Each tries to adopt the policy which it thinks will be most popular with the electorate. Elections are, of course, rather uncertain processes. There are many surprises, but the closer we get to the great day the clearer things become.

9. *The Swing.* Before each round of manoeuvring, an opinion poll is held. Appropriately, this is done by shuffling the election pack and dealing a card off the top. A black election card indicates that the swing is going in the opposite direction to that of the previous election. A red card or joker indicates that it is going in the same direction as the previous election. The election is held after three rounds of bargaining, before each of which a poll is held. The swing will be in the direction indicated by the majority of poll cards. In other words, if there are two or three black cards, then the swing will be in the opposite direction to that of the previous election; if there are not, then it will be in the same direction. Bear in mind that, since hearts have been removed from the pack, there is a 70 per cent chance that the swing will be reversed. Serious players may care to consult the more detailed analysis of probabilities at each stage in the process which can be found in the appendix to this chapter.

10. *Jockeying for position.* After the opinion poll card has been dealt at the start of each round, the parties will want to modify their policies in an attempt to capture as many votes as possible at election time. In each round of manoeuvring, party leaders

may move their marker (or not) in turn. It costs money to make a change of policy, however, since the electorate must be informed and convinced. Since small changes of policy are only to be expected, moving one space in either direction is cost-free. Each extra space moved costs the party £10 in campaign funds, which must be paid to the Bank. The parties may move as many spaces as they both want to and can afford (provided that the space which they land on is not already occupied by another party).

11. After each party has moved, or decided not to move, another opinion poll is held (as in rule 9). After this, another round of manoeuvring takes place. A third round of manoeuvring (preceded by a poll card) follows the second.

12. After three rounds of manoeuvring have taken place, the election is held. Each party must first pay £10 from campaign funds to the Bank to meet election expenses.

The election

13. The direction of the swing will already have been decided by the poll cards. A majority of black poll cards means that the swing goes in the opposite direction to that of the previous election, and the swing indicator must be moved accordingly.

14. The poll cards are then returned to the pack, which is reshuffled. The first results to be declared are those for the side of the board which will benefit from the swing. If the swing is to the right, then the first result to be declared is that for the policy space which is furthest to the right. If the swing is to the left, then the policy space furthest to the left is declared first. The results for the remaining policy spaces are declared in sequence, moving towards the centre of the board.

15. The result for each space is declared by dealing a card face up from the election pack.

IF IT IS A BLACK CARD, THEN VOTES WILL BE ADDED TO THE SUPPORT FOR THAT SPACE.

IF IT IS A RED CARD OR JOKER, THEN VOTES WILL BE TAKEN AWAY FROM SUPPORT FOR THAT SPACE.

IF IT IS AN ACE, 2, 3, 4, 5 ADD OR SUBTRACT 100 VOTES
IF IT IS A 6, 7, 8, 9, 10   „   „   „   200 „
„ „ „ „ COURT CARD   „   „   „   300 „
„ „ „ „ JOKER   „   500 „

After the result has been declared for each space, the counter above that space must be moved to indicate the new level of support.

16. The ten election cards which have been dealt are collected and *these cards only* are reshuffled. The results for the losing side of the board are now declared, starting with the most extreme position, by re-dealing these ten cards.

IF THE CARD IS BLACK, SUBTRACT THE APPROPRIATE NUMBER OF VOTES.
IF THE CARD IS RED, OR A JOKER, ADD THE APPROPRIATE NUMBER OF VOTES.

17. The level of support for each party can now be worked out. Each party receives all of the votes which are in columns nearer to its own policy position than to that of any other party. If there is an odd number of spaces between two parties, then the votes for the middle square are equally shared by the two parties concerned. (See examples below.)

18. The party with the most votes is declared the winner, and receives £100 from the Bank with which to conduct future campaigns. All other parties receive nothing.

19. Another election campaign starts immediately. The initial positions of the parties are those which they occupy as a result of the election which has just been held. Play therefore re-commences at rule 9. The winner of the last election makes the first move.

20. The winner is the party with the most money at the end of a specified time, or the only party left in the running if all others go bankrupt.

21. No policy space may, at any time in the game, receive more than 2000 votes or less than 100 votes.

22. *Ties.* Any tie between parties must be settled by a re-count.

Examples of election results

(i) An even number of spaces between adjacent parties

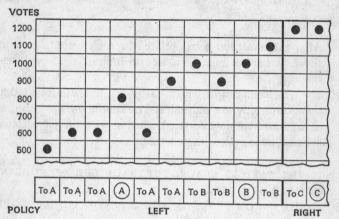

Party A's vote = 500 + 600 + 600 + 800 + 600 + 900 = 4000

Party B's vote = 1000 + 900 + 1000 + 1100 = 4000

(ii) An odd number of spaces between adjacent parties

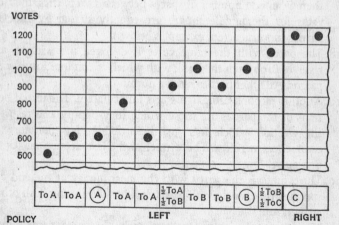

Party A's vote = $500 + 600 + 600 + 800 + 600 + \frac{1}{2}(900) = 3550$

Party B's vote = $\frac{1}{2}(900) + 1000 + 900 + 1000 + \frac{1}{2}(1100) = 3900$

Each party cuts the pack of election cards, and the highest card wins.

SOME VARIATIONS ON THE BASIC THEME

As always, it is open to the players to modify the rules as a majority of them sees fit. This section contains a few suggested ways to do this. For example, the election as it stands is held on the traditional British principle of 'first past the post'. The winner takes all, the losers take nothing. This can easily be modified if the players want to see the effects of other electoral systems. The payouts can, for example, be made according to the principles of proportional representation. In this case the £100 kitty is divided between the players in proportion to the votes that they received at the election, instead of being paid entirely to the winner. The total of all votes cast is calculated, followed by the percentage of votes received by each party. Each party then receives that percentage of the kitty (since the kitty is £100, this, of course, means that each party would receive £1 for every percent of the total vote). Alternatively, a more limited version of proportional representation can be introduced, whereby all parties getting less than 5 (or 10) per cent of the vote are excluded from the payout. An even more limited version is achieved by paying the first party £60, the second party £30, the third party £10 and the rest nothing. The implications of this sort of variation will be discussed below.

Other electoral systems can be simulated as well. For example, the French second-ballot system involves two successive elections, one between all the candidates, and another after eliminating the small parties (say those with less than 10 per cent) and anyone else who chooses to stand down. This is achieved by holding the election, then removing all parties with less than 10 per cent of the votes (keeping a note of the position they occupy) and allowing a five-minute recess for negotiations (and side payments) to decide on any further withdrawals. The votes are then simply re-counted and shared between the remaining parties.

Many other variations on the electoral theme can be attempted. The election results can be made more predictable, for example, by removing more red cards from the pack; conversely they can be made more unpredictable by inserting more red cards into it. Inserting additional red cards makes both the swing and the results of the election harder to predict, while taking red cards out has the opposite effect. Changing the predictability of the results influences competition between parties; the consequences of this will be discussed below.

You may feel that it is too easy or too difficult for parties to change their policies. This can be taken care of by increasing or decreasing the costs associated with moving spaces on the policy line. Alternatively a limit can be placed on the number of spaces which a party is allowed to move in one turn, or 'leapfrogging' over other parties can be charged at a higher rate.

If the game is played between teams, provision can be made for party splits by allowing any member of the team to set up shop on his own. This is achieved by placing a new marker on the board at a position which is initially adjacent to the original party. Alternatively two parties might be allowed to combine. They first move to adjacent ideological spaces and then take one of their markers off the board, dividing any subsequent profits between them according to an agreed formula.

Modifications of the type suggested above are always unpredictable in their consequences. A certain amount of trial and error is necessary to arrive at those variations which suit a particular group of players. Some modifications, such as introducing a system for enforcing agreements, will by now have been tried and tested.

HOW TO WIN ELECTIONS

You will soon discover that the initial declaration of party policy is an important part of the whole game. This is not because being outmanoeuvred early on means losing the election, but because recovering from being outmanoeuvred by *changing* your policy costs scarce campaign funds. The more money you use at this stage, the less you have available for winning elections later in the game. It should also be clear that having the first move is *not* an advantage. If you have to declare your policy early you are more likely to be outflanked; on the other hand, if you are able to listen to what everyone else has to say first you may find a way to outflank *them*. Therefore the first piece of advice is this : when cutting the cards, you should pray for an ace.

Maximum voting support is clustered at the centre of the policy scale, so you may be tempted to start off by placing your marker there. Bear in mind that the other players will think the same way. If you end up with another party directly on either side of you, you will be left with only those votes which directly correspond to your policy. Remember that the swing will go in one direction or another, so that support will increase on one side of the board or another when it comes to election time. You might want to take a gamble on a particular side, and try and get in there first. If you are declaring your policy relatively late in the day, you will have a lot more to go on. The really good places might already have been taken, but you will be able to see lucrative gaps in the policy spectrum where there is a group of voters which no one is trying to capture. You also run less of a chance of being outmanoeuvred by the players *moving after you.*

Consider adopting a policy at one extreme or the other of the scale. There are fewer votes to be won there overall, but the big advantage (particularly if the swing goes your way) is that you sweep up all of the votes on the extreme side of your position. If the swing does go in your favour, you will already be where you want to be, and will not have to spend campaign funds changing your policy. If the swing goes the other way you may even be compensated (as other players try and follow the movement of votes) by picking up some support on your other flank. In all circumstances you will want to avoid being boxed in by parties on either side of you taking up very similar policies to your own; getting out of this trap will cost money or lose votes.

Once the first opinion poll has been held, you will have some idea of the likely result of the election. If a black card is showing, there is a good chance that the swing will go in the opposite direction to that of the previous election (there is in fact only a one in seven chance that it will not). If the first card is red, be prepared for a swing in the same direction (the odds are now two to one that this will happen). Once you see which way the wind is blowing, you will want to change your policy to take account of likely election results. Be careful, and remember that moving more than one space costs money. The wind may change again, and moving back will cost still more money. If you feel sure of winning, of course, you can move quite a lot; the £100 prize will finance quite a lot of campaigning. However, you can never be really *sure* of winning, given the vagaries of the electoral system, so you will have to calculate the likely advantages in terms of an increased *chance* of being ahead at the finish.

As the election approaches, the incentives to move will increase. The swing will at some stage become a foregone conclusion (whatever happens this will be the case in the final round of manoeuvring). This will mean that the chances of having to change direction, spending funds and achieving nothing, will disappear. Once *you* make a move, of course, the *others* can move to take account of it, so you will still want to hang on as long as possible before making your final policy too obvious. The last move of all may well present you the hardest decision. You will have more information than at any other stage in the game, and there is no chance of being out-manoeuvred. You will be tempted to make a large and expensive move to the most promising position on the board (unless you are fortunate enough to be there already). However, the election results may upset everything, leaving you in a very poor position to fight subsequent campaigns. You may therefore decide to play it safe, in the knowledge that next time the swing is likely to come back in your direction. You give up your chances of winning this election but you save your thunder for the next time, when it might be more effective.

In general there are two basic styles of play which you can adopt. You can continually keep in touch with movements in electoral opinion, modifying your policies all the time to increase your chance of winning the current election. This will be expensive but may mean that you win more elections. Alternatively, you may stay put and conserve your campaign funds, waiting for a shift in opinion which favours you. You have a smaller chance of winning an election but fewer expenses. The decision on which style to play is partly a matter of preference, but also depends on what the other players are doing. If you win elections by hopping extravagantly around all over the place, you will win lots of money to hop around even more in the future. Splendid isolation may minimize your costs but you must not let the others get too far ahead of you. If you do this, even when things swing your way, your opponents will have sufficient funds to outflank you, even if it means hopping right across the board. By staying put and giving up the chance of winning you conserve your funds, but you are handing the election to someone else. This makes it easier for them to win again next time around.

Collusion between two or more parties can also be a very effective tactic. As always, side payments are allowed; if you think you are in a winning position, it is quite legitimate to pay one of the other players not to make a particular move, or perhaps to attack a dangerous opponent. Side payments might either take the form of a straight cash handout, or there might be a share of the potential winnings. They open up new sources of income for those who think that they have no hope of winning a particular election. These players can try to place themselves in a position where they are worth paying off or employing by another party.

One strategy which works well is for two adjacent parties to agree first of all to converge on each other and then to move slowly apart. They should not leave so large a gap between them that it becomes worth while for an opponent to try and split them by paying up and hopping into the middle, but should move far enough apart to ensure that a nice safe group of voters can be carved up between them. As always, no deals can be enforced unless by prior agreement of a majority of the players. Without some rule enforcing these inter-party agreements, the only thing encouraging either side to keep its word (bearing in mind that all of the profit is still paid to the winner), is the knowledge that continued cooperation in future elections may be more profitable in the long term than the benefits of a single double-cross in the short term.

Some of these strategies will have to be modified if any of the variations is introduced. If the proportional representation elections are introduced, deals will become more likely because they are easier to enforce. For the first time in this collection of games, payouts can be made to a *number* of players. Thus two who co-operate with each other will be able to do so in the knowledge that they both receive guaranteed rewards if their cooperation is successful. Side payments may still be offered to compensate for taking up a particularly bad position, but proportional payouts will mean that there will be many deals which are not undermined by each player's fear of being double-crossed. Proportional representation also removes some of the incentive to hop around the board, switching policy in search of *the* winning position. Under the first-past-the-post system, if you are a long way away from the action, your choice is between spending money to change a policy in exchange for *some* chance of winning, or staying put and giving up this election to conserve your campaign funds for next time. Under proportional representation rules your calculations are rather different since, even if you stay put, you may get *some* pay-off. The *extra* payoff you get from moving will be less than under first-past-the-post rules because the winner does not take the whole prize. The *costs* of *not being* the largest party are *smaller*, and the *benefits* of *being* the outright winner are *smaller*. You may well be less inclined to move, and this is clearly justified for each individual election. Bear in mind, however, that as long as other parties are winning more than you are, they are more likely to win the overall game. This is not only because the winner is the one with the most money, but because more money gives a party more flexibility, and therefore, by allowing it to change policy more often, makes it more likely to win further elections. You will almost certainly find that there are *fewer* policy changes in a proportional representation game. You will also find that the parties will be less inclined to bunch together around the area of maximum support. Often in a first-past-the-post game you will find that your best move is to go right up alongside another party, so that you share as few votes with it as possible; in the proportional representation game you will find that you may well do better staying further away from the others, thereby guaranteeing a smaller payoff, but reducing the risk of having all of your clothes stolen by someone else.

If a proportional system is introduced which only pays off the largest parties, then you will have to be a little more careful. You must make sure that your policies are popular enough to get you in among the winners. Your strategy will be somewhere in between that of pure proportional representation and first-past-the-post.

If you introduce a second-ballot electoral system then you will be *forced* to make deals if you want to have a hope of getting paid, either by the Bank or by another player. The Bank payout will be received by the player who is most successful at persuading adjacent candidates to withdraw and leave a wide range of voters who will be closer to him or her than to anyone else. You don't necessarily have to be in the best initial position to do this. You will receive the votes of those electors who are closer to you than to any other party, no matter where your policy lies, so that you can win by persuading all parties close to you to pull out. Since there is no further manoeuvring between the rounds of elections, it is quite possible that a policy position a long way from the action will end up winning, provided that other close competitors withdraw. This is because there is no chance of being outmanoeuvred by further policy shifts. The parties which withdraw will, of course, be back in the race at the same point in the next election.

Making the election results *more* predictable will probably make everyone *more* inclined to move around, since, for the same expenditure, the consequences are more clear-cut. There is less chance that a particular move will be rendered a waste of money by the election results. Greater predictability should also encourage policy changes earlier in the election campaign, since there is less chance that an apparent swing in one direction will subsequently be reversed. Making the election results *less* predictable will have the opposite effect. There will be a greater chance that swings will be reversed and a greater chance that, with a given swing, calculations will anyway be upset. A given change of policy will thus seem less obviously worthwhile, so that fewer such changes should take place. Paradoxically, greater uncertainty should make for a rather less lively game.

Finally, if party splits are allowed, particularly when combined with a proportional representation system of elections, a totally different set of game strategies emerges. Even *without* proportional representation, party splits make quite a difference. A particularly profitable possibility to consider is to split your party but to continue to collude with the breakaway faction. This enables you to 'spread' yourself further across the board. Instead of occupying a single point in the policy scale, you will occupy two points, as well as probably controlling all of the points between the two factions. This increases the chance that one of the parties has of winning. They will of course have to find some way of dividing the proceeds between them. Combinations of parties can also be profitable, especially in the first-past-the-post system. Two parties, neither of which has a hope of winning alone, might dramatically improve their chances of winning, and therefore of taking all the payout, by pooling their resources and voters. Once two parties have combined in this way, the others will probably start thinking of doing this as well, rather than risk being perpetual losers to a new and enlarged opponent. The advantages of combination are less clear in the proportional representation game, since not only do both parties get *something* anyway before they combine, but the prize which they stand to win after combination will also be less. Probably splits are more profitable under proportional representation rules, since each faction may do better on its own than it does sharing a single payout.

The basic rules of thumb are thus as follows. The more proportional the electoral system and the less certain the result, the more you should consider splitting but the less you should consider changing your policy. The less proportional the electoral system and the more certain the result, the more you should consider combining with others and frequently changing your policy.

REALITY

This game is rather more complex than the previous two, mainly because it is more explicitly concerned to be realistic. How realistic you think it is will depend on what you think of the fundamental assumption which underlies it. This is that politicians are primarily concerned to get elected, and will modify their policies as they see fit to achieve this end. The game operates as if politicians believe in policies only as long as these help them get elected but change their minds pretty quickly when they run out of luck. The game is not *quite* as cynical as this makes it sound, because it does allow for the possibility that politicians see themselves as having a duty to represent the wishes of the electorate, changing their policies when these wishes change, and measuring their success at doing this by the electoral success. The game does *not* incorporate the committed ideological politician, who participates in politics solely in order to enact particular policies, and is not prepared to compromise these things for any pragmatic consideration. Politicians are assumed to be trying to get elected by producing the most popular policies, either because they feel that this is their duty or because they want to get into power and are prepared to say anything at all to achieve this.

The game also assumes that politicians know *something* about the wishes of the electorate, and about how these change between elections. To simplify matters we only consider one issue, the level of income tax. This issue spreads the parties along the traditional left–right dimension which is a familiar way of describing British politics. Many other important political issues would array the parties along the same dimension, and these can be substituted if desired. These include the level of public expenditure, the amount of state intervention in the economy, the level of provision of various state-financed public services, the level of defence expenditure, and so on. Some important political issues cut across this dimension; recent examples include attitudes towards the European Economic Community, and towards devolution of power to Scotland and Wales. To represent all party policy as somewhere on a single left–right scale is obviously a considerable simplification. It is one, however, which makes the game a lot easier to play, while still capturing some of the essence of British party politics. Hardcore game players can complicate matters by playing the game simultaneously on a number of different boards, each representing an important policy. The final election result is arrived at by totalling the votes for each party on each board. This is letting things get a little bit out of hand, however. Games which go all out to represent real life get either boring or diabolically complicated.

This game, therefore, is played between politicians concerned to maximize their votes by modifying their policy on a single left–right scale. The consequence of this is that they will go where the voters are. This means that a lot of parties will want to be in the same place, particularly if the electoral system is first-past-the-post, which gives everything to the party with the most votes. If the game is played by only two parties, they will end up very close to each other in the centre of the board. Real two-party systems often tend to look like this, the protagonists adopting policies which are rather hard to tell apart. One explanation is that the assumptions which the game makes about politics are in fact right, and that politicians *are* mainly concerned to get as many votes as possible. With no other contenders to worry about, parties can neglect their more extreme wings, and drift towards the centre. Voters on the extremes will vote for them anyway, since this is the best that they can do. The place where votes are to be won is the centre, where they can be snatched from the grasp of the opposing party.

Add another party to the system and the pattern changes. Everyone still heads for the centre, but it becomes really bad news to be caught in the middle. Your two opponents grab the votes on either side, leaving you only with those electors who are really close to your own position. This is possibly why the centre always tends to be rather small in three-party systems. If there are more than three parties, the scramble for the centre becomes much less important. Parties spread themselves out across the range of policies because there is no incentive for those near the centre to move further in that direction. If they do this, they will only be followed by the parties on their more extreme flank, quite possibly losing more votes than they gain.

On the other hand, real party politics does not consist of endless changes of policy by each of the participants in an attempt to adapt to every slight shift in electoral opinion. Two things stop parties charging around all over the place. These are the cost of changing policies and the uncertainties involved in working out the best policy to adopt. The higher the cost, and the more the uncertainty, the less likely a change of policy. The cost to a party arising from changing its policies includes not only the costs of campaigning to tell voters what has happened, but also the loss of credibility a party suffers each time it makes a big policy shift. Other parties crow over broken promises, while voters start losing track of what the party really stands for. Every time the policy is changed, voters might get more and more convinced that the party does not mean what it says. In addition, in a changing world, there is always the chance that opinion will swing back in your direction, so that you can reap the benefit of new votes, as well as cashing in by boasting about your honesty and commitment to principles. The more uncertain the world is, the greater the chance that you will end up in this position by pure chance, and the less inclined you will be to waste hard-earned campaign funds on impressing the electorate.

One of the things which the game highlights is the effect of the electoral system on the policies put forward by the parties. The first-past-the-post system encourages parties to combine, both in the game and in reality, into larger and larger units in an attempt to increase the participants' chances of being the largest party at the end of the day. This is because the electoral system gives all of the goodies to the party with more votes than any other. The conclusion of this process is usually two parties confronting each other with roughly equal strength. This gives each an equal chance of getting the goodies, but makes neither that keen to go any further towards cooperation. Whatever happens, the first-past-the-post system tends to reduce the number of parties in the fight. We have seen that, if there is a small number of parties, they will tend to gravitate towards the centre when it comes to putting forward vote-catching policies. In short, first-past-the-post systems tend to have a few parties putting forward policies rather similar to each other and close to the centre of the ideological spectrum.

Proportional representation systems tend to do the opposite. The proportional representation game encourages parties to split, and provides them with few benefits if they combine. Thus the number of parties in the system tends to remain large. Furthermore, proportional representation tends not to encourage parties to solicit votes at any cost. Each party has *some* chance of getting in on the action as long as it gets *some* votes. Proportional representation systems encourage parties to offer a wider choice of policies to the electorate. Party policies tend to change less dramatically from election to election.

Finally, we turn to deals between parties. This is the hardest part to relate to reality because, while some deals between parties are made in public and judged by the electorate, many of the others are gentlemen's agreements made behind closed doors and never revealed to the public. The 'Lib-Lab Pact' which kept the 1974–9 Labour Government in power is a good example of a public deal, made 'over the counter' and exposed to the judgement of the electorate. Many profitable deals, however, cannot be made public because, if they were, the participants would almost certainly be punished at the next election. This is something which the game does not bring out. Such deals would include mutual agreement not to raise delicate issues which would damage both parties, or unpredictably damage one or the other party. They would extend to 'conspiracies of silence' on issues which are beyond the control of the parties, but which the electorate has strong feelings about. Most common, of course, are agreements to go easy on one particular issue in exchange for cooperation on another issue. This process of 'log-rolling' is fully explored in a later game.

APPENDIX: SWING PROBABILITIES AT EACH STAGE OF THE CAMPAIGN

The pack is assumed to contain no hearts and two jokers.

	No change in swing	Opposite swing
No opinion poll cards dealt	·30	·70
One black card dealt	·13	·86
One red card dealt	·62	·38
One red and one black card dealt	·36	·64

NB: There is no change in the swing if no more than one of the three opinion poll cards is black. Otherwise the swing is in the opposite direction to that of the previous election.

The probability that the outcome will be revealed in two cards is ·53.

5   Coalitions

A game for three to thirty players. It should take from 1 to 1½ hours.

The last game was about how we arrive at election results. This game is about what happens next. In most countries the fun isn't over after the results of the election have been declared. If no party controls a majority of the seats, we are still a long way from knowing who is going to form the government. Knowing that this is going to happen, the parties will obviously fight the election campaign rather differently. Chapter 6, Coalections, deals with this. This chapter focuses simply on the horse trading between political parties which takes place when each wants to get into the government, but none has a majority after the election. The governments which form must be coalitions, *combinations* of more than one party which do control a majority of seats. Coalition governments must not only control a majority of seats, however; they must also be able to agree upon how to divide the spoils of office, and upon government policy.

EQUIPMENT

1. A bundle of money.
2. A pack of election cards, produced by modifying an ordinary pack of playing cards as follows:
   (a) Remove all the tens, and two of the fives; leave in the jokers.
   (b) Court cards count zero, jokers count fifteen, aces count one and all other cards count at face value.
   (c) This produces a pack of forty-eight cards with a total face value of 200.
3. A blackboard or sheet of paper to display the election results.
4. Simple badges can be provided for each player to identify which party they represent.

THE RULES

1. Each player chooses a political party from the following list. If there are more than six players, they are formed into six teams.

   National Defence League (NDL)
   People's Revolutionary Alliance (PRA)
   Radical Socialists (RS)
   Progressive Party (PP)
   Reform Party (RP)
   Freedom Party (FP)

2. Each party is given £100 in 'operating expenses'.
3. *The election.* The election can be held as in the previous game (in which case see Chapter 4). If Coalitions is played on its own, a simple election can be held as follows. Each party pays £20 to the Bank. An equal number of election cards is then dealt to each party, face up, from the shuffled election pack. (Four parties will get twelve cards each, five parties will get nine cards each, six parties will get eight cards each.) Any remaining cards are discarded for this election, but shuffled into the pack before the next one. Each party wins as many MPs as the total face value of their hand, bearing in mind that court cards count zero, jokers fifteen, and all other cards at face value. Each calls out their number of MPs in turn and these results are displayed for all to see. The total number of MPs in the parliament is 200, or slightly fewer if five parties play, because three election cards are not used.
4. *Forming a government.* The players must now bargain with each other to decide which group of parties will form the government and share the rewards of office. The successful government coalition will receive a prize of £100 from the Bank to distribute to its various members. To take power (and win the prize) a coalition must therefore:
   (a) control more than half of the seats in parliament; that is, members of the coalition between them must control at least 101 seats (when five parties play, they still need 101 seats to form a government. The discarded seats are won by lunatic-fringe parties);

(b) reach an agreement between the members about how to divide up the prize.

Any coalition which can satisfy both of these conditions can take office and receive the prize. This prize will be paid out to coalition members as agreed by them before they took office.

5. *Organizing the bargaining.* There is no reason why the bargaining which takes place between the parties before a government is formed should not be as chaotic and disorganized as can be. More formal bargaining arrangements may be felt necessary, however. Two suggested alternatives are the public and private bargaining arrangements described below. If neither of these is adopted, a simple time limit should be imposed.

(a) Public bargaining. A time limit for the bargaining session is agreed in advance (say five or ten minutes). The player whose party has the largest number of seats makes a preliminary proposal for a government coalition which specifies the parties in the government, and the manner in which they will divide up the prize. This proposal may be provisionally accepted by the other proposed participants (they will be free to make alternative proposals later). If the proposal is provisionally accepted by *all* the proposed participants, then this coalition is now 'on the table' and stands until an alternative proposal is made and accepted by all of the participants in the new proposal. If the proposal is rejected by any of the participants in the proposed coalition, then there is 'no deal' on the table. Play moves in a clockwise direction. The next party is free to make a new proposal, or not. It may propose a coalition with different membership, a coalition with the same membership but a different division of the spoils, or 'no deal'. If another coalition proposal is made, then this must be accepted by all of the other participants, on the same basis as the previous proposals. If this happens, it becomes the current 'on the table' proposal. If a 'no deal' proposal is made, it must be accepted by a group of parties who between them control a majority of votes in the parliament. If it *is* accepted, 'no deal' becomes the current 'on the table' proposal.

During and between turns, players may communicate with

each other as they wish, although it is less chaotic if this communication is restricted to the passing of notes. Parties may make any side payments they wish with each other but, as always, no deals can be *enforced*.

At the end of the specified time, the proposal currently on the table takes effect. The prize is distributed to the members in the winning coalition in the proportions agreed in the proposal. If 'no deal' is on the table when the time limit expires, then no government forms, and another election must be held. Each player must pay the Bank a further £20 in election expenses, and £100 is added to the prize money at the next round.

(b) Private bargaining. A time limit for the bargaining session is agreed in advance (say five or ten minutes). During each bargaining session all players are free to communicate with each other as they wish, forming and re-forming into small groups and cabals. During this period, each party tries to negotiate a position for itself into the government coalition on the best possible terms. If the game is played by teams, there is no reason why different members of the teams should not negotiate independently. At the end of the time period, all talking must stop immediately. Each party must then write down the coalition which it wishes to propose, listing the members and the division of the prize between them. When everyone has written down a proposal, the papers are collected. If a winning government coalition has been proposed by all of its members, and if the division of the prize proposed is the same in all of these proposals, then that coalition forms and divides the kitty as agreed. If this does not happen, then no coalition is formed, another election is held, and £100 is added to the prize money for the next election.

6. *The payout*. The payout must be made to members of the winning coalition as agreed by that coalition before formation. If 'no deal' emerges (because no mutually acceptable coalition is proposed at the expiry of the time limit), then another election must be held. Each party must pay a further £20 to participate and £100 is added to the value of the next payout.

7. After the payout, another election is held immediately, with each player contributing a further £20. The process is continued, either until a pre-arranged time has elapsed, or until there are only two parties left in the game, at which point the party with the largest amount of money is the winner.

8. Variation A (see below) should be introduced after an agreed number of elections (say three to four).

9. *Party splits.* When the game is played by teams, the players may wish to split and control two separate parties. If one or more players want to leave a team and set up on their own they may do so. The resources of the old party are divided equally between the players. (Thus one player leaving a three-player team takes one third of the resources.) The new party must give itself a name, and can then be added to the scoreboard. It pays election expenses and receives an equal share of election cards as if it had always been in the game.

VARIATIONS ON THE THEME. SOME SUGGESTIONS

The following modifications should be among those considered for introduction under rule 8.

A. *Ideological bargaining.* This is an important modification, which should be introduced into all games of Coalitions once players have got the hang of the basic game: Government coalition members must also decide upon a policy for income tax. Each party has a different policy, and must compromise to get into the government. The policy of each party is decided as follows:

After the election each party totals the value of the *red* election cards in its hand. This value represents the rate of income tax (in per cent) which each party has promised to the voters that it will push for if elected to office.

Once a coalition forms, and becomes the government, it introduces a tax rate which has been agreed in advance by the members. Each party in the coalition must pay a penalty for every percentage point which government policy deviates from its own policy. This is to compensate for the electoral disadvantage suffered by parties who promise electors one thing, and then go into governments which do something else. The penalty is £2 for every 1 per cent difference between government policy and party policy, and only applies to members of the winning coalition. These penalties are paid to the Bank as soon as the coalition takes office.

   More complicated games can be produced by giving each party a *number* of policies. Each policy is determined by the value of each suit in the hand of election cards. Hearts represent welfare policy, clubs represent defence policy, spades represent public works policy, and diamonds represent industrial policy.

B. The two jokers become *personality cards*, each representing a political *prima donna* who will not share the limelight with another. No government coalition may form which includes both. If one party holds both cards, it is hopelessly split, and cannot participate in a coalition until the next election.

C. Members of the winning coalition may choose to keep up to four of their election cards for the next election. If they do this, all remaining cards are returned to the pack, which is shuffled. Those players retaining cards will receive enough new cards to make up the necessary total.

HOW TO WIN COALITIONS

You will probably have detected an underlying similarity with Primitive Politics when playing this game. There is a clear need to combine cooperation with the other players (without which no governments can be formed and no prizes won) with the conflict which arises because, at the end of the day, there is only one winner. Coalitions is a game which forces players to balance these mixed motives. While you want to make as much as you can for yourself, you must offer enough to the other players to make sure that they want to do business with you. There will always be several winning coalitions for any given election result. You may want to rule some of these out straight away. For example, you don't gain very much by including parties whose votes are not essential in winning coalitions. These parties are passengers, not adding to the resources of the coalition yet expecting a share of the payout. Once passengers have been eliminated you will still have a number of potential coalition partners to choose from. If you are in a coalition which is just winning, you can always form another winning coalition by defecting and getting together with all of the other parties. Since these other parties risk getting nothing at all, they will probably listen quite hard to what you have to say. Of course, every other party in the original coalition will be in the same position as you are, and will also be trying to do a deal with the outsiders. Imagine that you are in a three-party coalition which carries no passengers yet controls a majority of the seats. You agree among yourselves to split the prize three ways. If there are two other parties in the game who stand to get nothing, you could approach them and offer to go into government with them if they take £10 each (better than nothing) and leave you with the remaining £80. Another member of the original coalition, who is now in danger of being cut out of the payoff, could beat that by offering the outsiders £20 each and taking £60. You, or someone else, could counter this by offering them £30 each and taking £40. This process can go on and on; there is no natural stopping point. Every offer which can be made can be bettered. The bargaining *would* go on and on if there was nothing to stop it. There is something to stop it, however – the time limit. If no deal is arranged by the time that this expires, all the players get nothing.

You can try three ways of getting out of this problem. The first way is to try and form longer-term agreements with other parties. You might agree to keep going into coalition with them, whatever short-term inducements are offered by their opponents. If you agree with another party to behave as a single unit, only going into and coming out of coalition together, you can greatly increase your bargaining power. By standing or falling as one, you can increase that chance that together you can present other players with a take-it-or-leave-it offer, since you will not be competing with each other for their favours. Sometimes this type of long-term agreement may force you to break the maxim that coalitions shouldn't carry passengers. It is quite possible that either partner alone becomes necessary for a particular majority, but both of you would be too many. In this case, you may agree for partners to go into the government and pay the other off from the winnings; or you might insist that either both partners are included in the coalition or neither.

Another way of attempting to increase your chances of being in the winning coalition, and short-circuiting the endless bargaining process, is to look for weak partners. The less crucial a particular party is, the less it is likely to receive lucrative offers from your opponents. If a particular party is necessary to your coalition, it will always be necessary to someone else's as well, but the fewer alternative coalitions a party can join, the more carefully it will listen to what you have to say.

Finally, you might press for the introduction of private bargaining. The differences between private and public bargaining will be discussed below, but it should be clear that rivals can only better an offer if they know what it is. The arrangements for private bargaining make this impossible. Even if the party which you are trying to seduce tells a rival what you have offered, it can never be sure of being believed. It might always be lying in order to bid up alternative offers. Private bargaining may therefore bring some stability to the bargaining although, as we shall see, it has other disadvantages.

As you play the game you will quickly realize that the relationship between the number of seats which you win at each election and your bargaining power is rather more complicated than it seems at first sight. Your bargaining power is based upon your ability to make threats. These threats usually take the form 'if you don't give me what I'm asking for, I'll go off and make a deal with someone else'. The more threats like this you can make, the stronger your position and the greater your bargaining power. This bargaining power is therefore related to the number of coalitions of which you are an essential member. The more coalitions you can smash up by leaving, the stronger you are. This power can change very erratically. For example, if the game is played between three players and each has about the same number of seats, they will all be equally powerful. None will be able to form a government alone, yet each will be able to form a government in coalition with either of the others. Each will have the same number of threats to make, and therefore the same amount of power. Suppose you do very badly at the next election, losing support equally to your two rivals. Even a disastrous electoral performance might leave you no worse off in terms of bargaining power. Say you end up with only 10 out of 200 seats, while the others have 95 each. As a matter of fact, your bargaining power is unchanged. It still takes two parties to form a government, and any two will do. There is no reason, therefore, why you should take a smaller share of the payout than before. You are just as important as before to any coalition which forms. There is still only one coalition which works without you, and two which need your support.

On the other hand, very small changes in your parliamentary representation can have quite dramatic effects on your power. Imagine a game played between four parties. At one election each has 50 seats and obviously each has the same amount of power. At the next election you lose 2 seats, 1 each to two of the other parties. This leaves you with 48 seats, and the others with 51, 51 and 50. You lose a lot of bargaining leverage. In fact you have no bargaining power at all, since you are now redundant to any coalition which might form. Any two of the other parties can form a winning coalition of at least 101 seats. Any winning coalition which you are a member of would still be winning if you left, so you do not have much to threaten the others with. Anything you can get in this situation is jam. Thus, while you could lose (or gain) a large number of seats and end up with the same bargaining power, you could also lose (or gain) a very small number of seats and lose (or gain) a very large amount of bargaining power.

This process becomes even more subtle after you add the rule which makes coalition partners decide on a policy for income tax as well as deciding on the share-out of the prize. Because each party must pay a penalty for each percentage point on which party policy differs from coalition policy, and because each party will have a different policy, some coalitions will now be 'worth' more than others. Before the players had to bargain over policies, every coalition was worth the same amount, £100. Once the parties must pay penalties for agreeing to policies which are not their own, each coalition is bound to be worth less than £100 (unless all members happen to have the same policy). The total value of the penalties must be deducted from the total value of the coalition. This makes coalitions between groups of parties with similar policies more attractive than coalitions between groups of parties with widely differing policies. Diverse coalitions will always have to pay heavier penalties than compact ones. Parties should therefore look for partners with rather similar policies to their own if they want to increase the likely payoff. This affects the bargaining power of all concerned. We have seen that your power will depend upon the threats which you can make. Obviously a threat to leave a coalition in which you stand to pay a small penalty in order to join a coalition in which you stand to pay a large penalty has less impact than a threat to leave an expensive coalition and join a cheap one. Your bargaining power will be partly determined by your policy. This makes it more attractive to have a policy pretty much in the middle of the range of policies held by the other parties. Quite frequently a small party in the centre of the range is much more powerful than a similar party at one extreme of the range. The party at the extreme will have very little choice of viable coalition partners while the party in the centre will have the pick of quite a few. It can even be the case that a small party near to the centre can do better than a large party at the extreme. The importance of this factor can obviously be modified by changing the rate of the penalty. The greater the penalty, the greater the relative advantage for parties in the centre. The lower the penalty, the less this relative advantage.

The third thing which we have already seen affects the way you play is the type of bargaining arrangements which are in force. Chaotic bargaining, with no formal arrangement other than a time limit, may be hard on the eardrums, but can really suit the sophisticated operator. Keeping your head while all around you are losing theirs may be just the way to fool your friends into all sorts of awful deals. As the time limit approaches they may be prepared to take anything rather than nothing. There will be two basic things that you will be trying to do. On the one hand you will be trying to get into coalitions on the best terms possible. On the other hand you will be trying to stop coalitions forming of which you are not a member. We have already talked a bit about the first, but don't neglect the second. It can be just as important. If no coalition forms there is a new election and the stakes are doubled. If things begin to look bad for you, try and confuse matters by making mischievous offers to the others aimed at breaking up coalitions in which you are not included, without leaving them time to re-form before the time limit expires. That gives you a second chance to win the prize money, with nothing lost. If this happens too often, some of the players will certainly try to organize the chaos in order to reduce the scope for mischief-making.

Public bargaining, with all deals out in the open, produces a climate in which it is much harder to bamboozle people. You've got to make a real offer which, if accepted, stands a chance of actually coming about. Opportunities for wheeling and dealing do still emerge as the time limit approaches, when you can try to hurry people into accepting any deal rather than no deal, or into accepting no deal and doubling the stakes for the next game.

Private bargaining is the most complex of all, because all of the participants in the winning coalition must agree on the precise membership and the precise division of the spoils in their secret proposal at the end of each round. This means that you never quite know what deals have been arranged by the others behind your back. They might have agreed a completely different coalition amongst themselves, leaving you out in the cold to make a ridiculous proposal and lose everything. On the other hand, you can try and do the same thing to them or simply defect from a coalition which you don't like, leaving 'no deal' and double stakes for the next game. Opportunities for such tricks are considerably increased when the game is played by teams. Representatives of the same party can be talking to different people at the same time. Between them, these representatives can try and offer a deal to everyone, getting together at the end of the session to select the best of the bunch.

We've already seen that longer-term deals between parties to cooperate can greatly improve the prospects of the participants. Of course, a number of strategies which have just been considered must be modified if long-term deals emerge. Sometimes both participants will not be necessary together in any coalition, so that it might be necessary for one or more of them to be left out in the cold. When the personality cards are introduced it is quite possible that two participants in a deal will each have a card, prohibiting them from going into government with each other. Finally, once policy bargaining is introduced, two participants in a deal may find themselves after a particular election with widely differing policies. In these cases, some form of side payment will be necessary to maintain the deal. If the participants do not much trust each other, they may try to introduce some means of enforcing agreements, while their opponents may try to block this if they feel that it increases the chances of profitable cooperation between their opponents.

Whatever happens, there is only one winner. This means that, as in all the games, any cooperation will be based entirely on self-interest. You can't win without cooperation, so the basic principle of play must be to give away just enough to tempt the others into alliances with you, being careful not to give away so much that you are open to being double-crossed in the show-down.

REALITY

The British are unused to coalitions, and regard them with intense suspicion. The 'winner-takes-all' electoral system underlies a winner-takes-all attitude towards the division of the spoils of office. Politicians belonging to the two major parties clearly prefer to have all of the power some of the time than some of the power most of the time, and these attitudes will clearly be with us for a long time. Nevertheless, most other European countries have been governed by coalitions at some stage in their post-war history, mainly because it would have been impossible for one party to go it alone. Even in Britain the 1974–9 parliament saw a minority Labour government retaining office for most of that time only through a 'pact' with the Liberals which was concluded as a result of a number of significant policy concessions. Some British local politicians will be more familiar than their parliamentary colleagues with the trials and tribulations of being forced to cooperate with other parties.

The City of Liverpool, for example, has had no majority party for some time. While Liverpool has not yet had a *formal* coalition administration, the fate of each issue has been decided by a sequence of volatile agreements between each of the three main parties. None could go it alone, but any two parties could force through any measure if they joined forces.

As far as government coalitions are concerned, any agreement between parties must include statements on two major matters. These are the distribution of seats between parties in the cabinet, and the precise policies to be adopted on each major issue which is likely to arise. In the game, the cabinet is represented by the fixed prize awarded to the successful coalition. The fact that the prize is fixed, and the fact that everyone is trying to make as much money as possible, means that winning coalitions will not tend to carry passengers whose votes are not essential to the survival of the government. In reality, there are two things which make the game an over-simplification. Firstly, it is not always necessary for a government to command a majority of votes in the parliament for it to receive the benefits of office. Minority governments have formed in the past and will no doubt form in the future. This is usually because the opposition is sufficiently divided not to be able to agree on bringing a particular government down, or because the various opposition parties do not see any electoral advantage, and quite possibly see electoral disaster, in destroying every government that does not have a majority. In the unmodified game minority governments cannot form. One modification which might go some way towards accommodating the real-life possibility of minority governments would be to give half of the prize to the largest single party in the event of 'no deal' emerging. While minority governments do tend to be the largest party in a particular system, this is by no means invariably the case, however.

In addition to this, it is not unheard of for real coalition governments to carry passengers, parties whose votes are not necessary for a parliamentary majority. There are three probable reasons for this. The first can be found in the game: longer-term agreements between two or more parties to cooperate come what may are not always dissolved simply because they are not all necessary to a particular majority. Indeed this is part of the essence of such agree-ments. Furthermore, coalition governments will often not want to govern with a bare majority of the seats in a parliament, because they are not sure of their supporters or because they fear the con-sequences of defections on particularly embarrassing issues. These coalitions take on board some extra support as insurance. This allows government parties to 'go their own way' on particular issues which they feel really strongly about, without risking the life of the government. In other words a working majority may be rather larger than a straightforward 50 per cent + 1 of the seats in the house. Another reason for building a larger majority than you really need at the beginning of the life of a particular government is that governments expect some erosion of their position as indi-vidual parliamentarians defect from the party, as the government parties loose seats in by-elections, and so on. This process of decay can be accommodated in the game by raising the number of seats which the government party must control from 101 seats to, say, 110 or 120.

Finally, in times of national crisis, governments of 'national unity' are sometimes formed in which all sides bury the hatchet to get the country out of trouble. Obviously, in these circumstances, government coalitions include passengers. This possibility is obvi-ously not included in the game.

Having allocated cabinet responsibilities, the other important matter which coalition partners must agree upon before they can form a government is their policy on the important issues of the day. The game includes one such issue, although intrepid gamesters could add others. Both in the game and in reality, the need to agree a government policy means that coalitions of parties which have similar policies will be preferred to coalitions of parties which have policies which are wildly different. In the game parties are simply *given* policies; in reality, of course, they have some control over them. The important point which the game illustrates is that a party's power, its ability to get into the government, will be affected not only by its size but also by its policies. Large parties with extreme policies may be able to extract much less out of the system than small parties with policies which make them attractive coalition partners. This means that, if parties want to get into power, the possibility of coalition governments will encourage parties to modify their policies in such a way that they appeal to as many of the others as possible.

The combined effects of party strength and party policy illustrate some of the fascinating intricacy of coalition bargaining. We saw that a large change in a party's support might have a very small effect on its bargaining power and, conversely, that a very small change in support might have a very large effect on power. There is no clear evidence that real political parties exploit their bargaining advantages to the utmost, with very small parties getting as big a slice of the cake as very large ones when both are equally necessary to a particular coalition. The *possibility* of a small party holding large parties to ransom is, however, something which clearly worries those people who oppose the introduction of proportional electoral systems, since proportional systems often produce coalition governments. Of the many arguments against proportional representation and coalition government (most of them very bad) this is the most sophisticated. The point is basically that, instead of seriously *under-representing* small parties with a 'winner-takes-all' system, we seriously *over-represent* them with proportional representation. This is not because proportional representation gives small parties more seats than they deserve, but because giving a small party even its fair share of seats can sometimes allow it to wield a disproportionate amount of power. The game should give the players some insight into this argument, which becomes even more troublesome when party policy is considered. Since parties with policies which are close to those of a number of their rivals will be in a relatively strong position when it comes to forging a coalition platform, it follows that small parties near the centre of the spectrum will be better placed to get into government than small parties on the extremes. The game illustrates the *potential* power of small centre parties quite clearly. The validity of this as an argument against proportional representation depends, of course, on the extent to which this potential power is, in practice, exploited. The fact remains that, in theory, a small centre party can find itself in a surprisingly strong position in coalition negotiations.

Finally, we saw that the particular bargaining arrangements adopted can have a big impact in the process of coalition formation. Different countries vary considerably in the extent to which coalition bargaining is conducted in public, and the game illustrates that this factor can have considerable implications. In the real world it is possible that completely cynical wheeling and dealing will be punished by the electorate. This sort of behaviour is more unlikely in the game the more public the bargaining process, and in real-life politics public mischievousness is even more likely to be unproductive. The more private and the less controlled the bargaining process, the greater the chance of peculiar deals and of not reaching any agreement at all, and it is certainly true that the possibility of 'government in smoke-filled rooms' is one of the main arguments used by opponents of coalition politics.

Whatever else, the basic mixture of conflict and cooperation is clearly present in real coalition bargaining. Parties want to get into government, and to do so must make compromises in the knowledge that the compromises they make could turn out to be very damaging. In certain circumstances, the compromises may appear to be potentially so dangerous that the party gives up all hope of getting into power in a particular session, contents itself with opposition, and bides its time until the next election. Somewhere between total aggression and total compliance lies the ideal bargaining posture for hopeful coalition members. A given number of seats in the parliament, and a given policy, may leave your party in an unexpectedly good, or an unexpectedly bad, bargaining position when the power and policies of the other parties are taken into consideration. These paradoxes of power underlie coalition politics both in the game and in reality.

6   Coalections

A game for three to thirty intrepid players. It should take from
1½ to 2 hours.

This game, which is a combination of the previous two games, sets
out to show the ways in which future coalition governments can
influence election campaigns. The parties in Elections want only to
get as many seats as possible in parliament, regardless of consequences after the election. The parties in Coalitions want to squeeze
as much as possible out of each coalition, regardless of what might
happen at the next election. In real life these two processes cannot
be separated. Coalections forces players to balance coalition advantage against electoral disadvantage, and vice versa. The game is
similar to Coalitions. The main difference is that the election results are determined by playing a round of Elections.

THE RULES

1. Exactly the same equipment is used as for the game of Elections.
2. The game is set up in exactly the same way as for the game of
   Elections (see p. 46).
3. The election campaign and the election itself are conducted
   according to the rules for the game of Elections (rules 5–17,
   pp. 48–51).
4. The election results are determined using a proportional representation system. The total size of the electorate at the start of
   Elections is 19,800 votes. For each 100 votes a party wins at the
   election, it receives 1 seat in the parliament. The largest party is
   awarded 2 additional seats. Fractions of 100 votes give no seats.
   (The electorate may shrink a little bit during the game. Votes
   lost because of this are won by wildcat parties who will go into
   no government.) The total number of seats in the parliament is
   therefore 200.

5. Once the election results have been calculated, seat totals for each party are displayed on a blackboard.
6. The parties must now form a coalition government in order to collect a share of the £100 prize. The coalition government must
   (a) control more than half of the seats in parliament; that is, members of the coalition between them must control at least 101 seats;
   (b) reach an agreement between the members about how to divide up the prize;
   (c) Reach an agreement between the members on a government policy on income tax.
7. Each party's policy on income tax is that indicated by its position on the Elections board. These policies range from 60 per cent on the extreme left of the board to 22 per cent on the extreme right. If a party goes into government, it must forfeit £2 for every 1 per cent difference between its own policy on income tax and that agreed by the coalition. These penalties are paid to the bank as soon as the coalition takes office.
8. The bargaining which precedes the formation of the coalition is conducted in exactly the same way as in the game of Coalitions (pp. 66–8).
9. Once the coalition has formed, or once the time limit has elapsed and no deal has emerged, there is another election, conducted as described above. If no deal emerges, the prize at the next election is increased by £100.

HOW TO WIN COALECTIONS

Many of the techniques described in the previous two chapters can be brought to bear on Coalections. There are, however, a number of very important differences.

Consider the election campaign first. When playing Elections the aim of each party was to get as many seats as possible. Whatever electoral system was used, getting more seats increased the chances of a large payout. This had to be balanced against the costs of changing party policy in order to attract more votes. In Coalections the payout is not made automatically to *any* party. Even the largest party may well end up with nothing if enough of the others combine against it. Parties fight elections in order to increase their bargaining power in the subsequent coalition negotiations. We have already seen that this bargaining power increases in rather peculiar ways. While you can never make yourself worse off by getting more seats, you may well end up no better off while sometimes just a few more seats can dramatically increase your power. If changing your policy to increase your votes did not cost anything there would be no problem, but changing your policy costs money. You will not want to spend money increasing your votes if those extra votes give you no more power. On the other hand some small policy changes, costing relatively little, might reap even richer returns in power than they do in votes. Consider the examples used in the previous chapter. If there are three parties, all with about the same number of votes, you must improve your election results spectacularly to get any more power. In fact you have to do so well that you end up with more than half of the seats all on your own. In these circumstances you might feel disinclined to spend money on attracting more votes unless you thought that you could do just that. Anything else would be money down the drain. You would get more votes, but so what? If there are four parties, however, and the other three have just over 50 seats each, while you have just under 50 seats, you will be left out of *any* coalition. You really must do better at the next election, and even a very small advance may well put you in the money. Instead of having to win the 30-odd seats needed in the previous example before your power goes up, 2 or 3 extra seats might be enough to produce a considerable improvement in your bargaining position. In this case any money spent on getting those vital extra seats would be very well spent.

If only things were as simple as that. But getting more votes means changing your policy. As well as costing you money in the election campaign, changing your policy will affect the payout you get if you get into a coalition. This is because you must pay a penalty if your policy is not the same as that of the coalition. Furthermore your policy affects your attractiveness to other likely coalition partners. The closer your policy is to theirs, the more they will want to go into government with you. Your policy therefore affects your bargaining power as well as your payout. All of this means that there are several more reasons which might make you want to change your policy at election time, each of which has nothing to do with how many votes you get. You might want to change your policy so that it is closer to that of other parties because this makes you a more attractive coalition partner and therefore makes you more powerful. You guess at which coalition will form, guess at the policy which it will decide on, and try and get as close to this as possible. This means that, if you are included in the government, you will have to pay as small a penalty as possible. Changing your policy has become a very complicated decision. There are four main factors which you must take into consideration, but any move you make will often help you in some ways and harm you in others. Actually working out the costs and benefits of a particular move becomes extremely complicated, given all of the uncertainties involved. You will have to begin to play by 'feel'.

To summarize, the main effects of a change in your tax policy will be:

(a) It will increase your votes, but cost you money in election expenses. This may be worth it in the short term but not in the long term, may be worth it in the long term but not in the short term, or may not be worth it at all. (See 'How to win Elections', p. 54 ff.)
(b) It may or may not increase your bargaining power, even if you increase your seat total. Some small gains help you a lot, some large gains are useless. All moves cost money.
(c) It will affect your payout when you get into a coalition. It might be worth making your free move of one space to achieve this; it is never worth paying money if this is your only gain. Each extra space costs £10 to move, but can only save you £4 in penalties. This might, however, be an additional incentive to make a move about which you are undecided.
(d) It will affect your attractiveness as a coalition partner, which affects your chances of sharing in the payout at all.

It is quite possible that a particular change in policy may increase your seats and bargaining power, but move you further away from likely coalition partners. This would make you less attractive to others, and cost you more money in penalties if you succeed in getting into government. On the other hand, it is equally possible that a move which *loses* you votes might be a good one, because it does not damage your bargaining power very much, yet makes you a more attractive partner. Despite the fact that you have fewer seats, you might be more likely to get into the government as a result of a particular change of policy. In Coalections, small can be beautiful if what you say sounds good to the others.

The other major difference between Coalections and the previous games is in the nature of the deals which you might make with other parties. The likelihood of deals is now much greater. Parties will want to coordinate their policies to get the most out of being in government, yet will want to make sure that opponents do not capitalize on this. As far as coalitions are concerned, parties should ideally place themselves right next to each other on the policy scale, so that they pay very few penalties when they get into government. This, however, will leave the next election wide open for those parties who are not in the government, who can move around and capture large numbers of votes. On the other hand, election deals usually involve agreeing to keep your distance from the others and not encroaching on their support as long as they return the favour. These deals can be rather expensive when it comes to forming a government.

Opposition parties will be faced with similar dilemmas. If the government parties huddle together with similar tax policies, there will be a temptation to charge around the board at election time, picking up votes from all and sundry. Every party's object, however, is to get into government. Charging around the board might be fine at election time, but the chickens will come home to roost when it comes to forming a ruling coalition. This increases the incentives for *opposition* parties to do a deal with each other. If they do not cooperate, then they will be hampered in their campaign to attract votes from the government parties by the fact that they are also in competition with each other. If they come to some arrangement, then they can group themselves together and coordinate an election campaign which wins votes but does not leave them paying heavy penalties when it comes to forming a government. Thus, if a stable deal between government parties seems to be emerging, those who are on the outside should immediately consider similar cooperation.

The other major alternative for the opposition parties is to attempt to seduce a member of the government by promising very favourable terms after the next election. As you will have seen from playing Coalitions this can quickly result in chaos, setting off a flurry of bids and counter-bids. This might be just what the opposition wants. Breaking up the government coalition is the clear alternative to beating it at the next election.

REALITY

Real-life coalition governments have to conduct themselves with several of their many eyes on the next election. Parties tend to get lumbered with the policies of coalitions of which they are part. Indeed the final straw that breaks the back of a particular government is often when one of the members is faced with accepting a particular policy which it knows spells electoral disaster. Similarly, when parties know that there will be a coalition government, their electoral campaigning is tempered by the knowledge that, at the end of the day, they are going to have to come to some form of agreement with at least some of their current opponents.

Finding the best all-round policy in these circumstances is a very complex business, particularly because the punishments which the electorate has up its sleeve are often so imponderable. In part this is because parties often believe that there is another very important thing which impresses voters, and which the game does not capture. This is an image of 'responsibility' fostered by not frivolously breaking up governments and not going into deals which you have no intention of keeping. For example, the Liberal Party went into a sort of semi-coalition with Labour in Britain to keep the 1974–9 government alive despite the fact that it knew that *any* policy shift which it might make would lose its voters. If it moved leftwards towards Labour it would lose its rightish support while picking up nothing in return; if it moved right, towards the Tories, and brought the government down, it would lose its leftish supporters.

Faced with having to bring the government down or keep it in power, the Liberals were on a hiding to nothing in terms of policy, and chose to keep Labour in power probably because they felt that the responsible image that this might create would at least offset some of their losses. There is a popular belief, at least among some politicians, that voters punish the party or parties which they hold responsible for dragging them out to the polling booths.

Not surprisingly, real life is more complex than the game, but the aim of the game is to highlight at least some of the rather odd things which can happen in election campaigns when the result is bound to be some sort of coalition. For example, even if we think of politicians as solely concerned with their own welfare, we should not necessarily expect them always to adopt the most vote-catching policies. If they do something which loses votes, we do not have to conclude necessarily that they mean what they say, or that they have made a mistake. It could well be that some of the more subtle interactions between trying to get into a coalition and trying to get elected have come into play. We have seen that moves which make it more likely that you will end up in the government might lose you votes but, if you end up better off, why worry? On other occasions parties may refuse to make what seem to be really obvious moves to capture a section of support which nobody else is catering for. This can be because a policy shift would net more votes but would not help, and might even hinder, coalition chances.

Playing the game you will also see some of the advantages and disadvantages of pacts and deals between parties. Deals can help you solve some of the problems which arise because elections make you want to do one thing, while coalitions make you want to do something else. If two parties agree not to take advantage of each other at election time, each can have a much easier time adjusting coalition policy to please everyone. However, each is open to exploitation by the opposition. If there is no deal and it's a free-for-all at election time, it is easier to keep the opposition at bay, but more difficult when it comes to rebuilding the government. In practice both things happen. Sometimes a coalition government will go to the electorate united and ask for a mandate to continue. How they actually go about doing this will depend on the method of holding elections. They might, for example, put up a single candidate from the strongest government party in each area. This is what tends to happen in the French second ballot. Alternatively, given certain proportional systems, all parties might stand in each area, but urge the voters to give additional support to their coalition partners. This has happened in the Irish Republic. On the other hand, many coalition governments simply break up and fight each election as completely independent parties, even if there is a vague intention to reconstitute the coalition after the election campaign is over. Each party then has a chance to try and increase its bargaining power relative to the other members of the coalition, in order to try and get a larger proportion of the cabinet, or to force government policy in its direction.

Real governments have a lot more to agree than a single rate of income tax, of course. One of the most important ways in which coalition governments can come to terms with the conflicting desires of members can only be captured by making the game even more complicated. When a number of parties must make compromises on a number of issues, an obvious solution is to let each have its own way on those issues which it feels most strongly about, or on which its electoral support is based. Thus a coalition between a social democratic party, a nationalist party and a religious party has a lot of scope for making concessions without taking too many electoral risks. Religious policy comes close to that of the religious party, regional policy comes close to that of the nationalist party, and social policy comes close to that of the social democratic party. So each party can get its way on the issue which most impresses its own electorate. This can be accomplished by modifying the game as suggested in the discussion of Elections (p. 61). Several election boards could be used, each representing policy on a particular issue, with parties paying penalties only for the amount which their policy on the board on which they got the most votes differs from coalition policy. This can be quite complicated and an easier way to develop a feel for some of the complexities of this process is to give up at this point and go on to the next game, Rolling Logs, where trade-offs between different policies are the essence of what is going on.

A game for five to thirty players. It should take from 1 to 1½ hours.

The previous games, when they have been concerned with political *issues*, have made one important simplification; they have dealt with only one issue at a time. In the real world, much of the political wheeling and dealing which takes place is about playing one issue off against another. In this game, the players are members of a committee which must take decisions on matters of policy concerning four basic issues. The balance of opinion will usually be such that no one issue will have a majority of committee members supporting it. Those in favour will have to enlist the support of some who are opposed. The trick is to make these people an offer they can't refuse. This usually involves supporting them on *their* pet issue, in exchange for their help on yours.

EQUIPMENT

1. A bundle of money.
2. A watch.
3. Two packs of playing cards:
   (a) The first pack has all court cards and jokers removed, and is known as the *agenda pack*.
   (b) The second pack contains all its cards, as well as the court cards and jokers from the agenda pack. All court cards count as additional jokers. This pack is known as the *preference pack*.

THE RULES

1. If there are more than nine players, they are formed into between five and nine teams. Each team is provided with £100.

2. First we decide the attitude of each player on each of the issues. This is done by shuffling the preference pack and dealing an equal number of cards to each player or team, until there are fewer cards than players left. The remaining cards are discarded for that round, face down. The hand of cards received by each player or team tells them their preference on each issue. Each issue is represented by a suit in the pack as follows:

Hearts represent social security.
Clubs represent defence.
Diamonds represent industry.
Spades represent public works.

The more cards a player has in a particular suit (and the more high cards in that suit) the more likely it is that he will be rewarded if the committee decides to spend money on that issue. All court cards and jokers represent votes against *any* issue (see below), and their suit is irrelevant.

3. Before the committee goes into session, we must decide the agenda, the issues to be discussed and the order of their discussion. This order is always full of surprises, and is fixed by dealing twelve cards in a line from the shuffled *agenda pack*. The first card is dealt face up, the next face down, the next face up, and so on. The suit of each card in the agenda represents the issue which will be discussed at each stage in the meeting. If the first card is a heart, the first issue will be social security, if the first card is a diamond, the first issue will be industry, and so on.

4. The committee now goes into session, and starts to discuss the first item on the agenda. A project concerning the issue under discussion is up for consideration. The decision to spend money or not on this project is taken by a majority vote of all members of the committee.

5. There is a three-minute negotiating session before each project is voted upon. The players are free to discuss with each other how they are going to vote, to show each other cards from their hand, and even to buy and sell cards from each other. They will bear in mind (see below) that only the players who hold seven, eight, nine and ten cards in a particular suit will make a profit if

the vote goes in favour of the relevant issue. Those holding these high cards will try to put together a majority on this basis.

6. At the end of the three-minute period, the committee moves to a vote on the issue in question. Voting is accomplished by each player placing a card from his hand face down on the table, not letting anyone else see the card which he is playing. Votes against a motion are cast by playing a joker or court card. Votes in favour of a motion are cast by playing any other card. Thirty seconds are allowed for the voting. Any player not casting a vote within this period pays a £10 forfeit, and is deemed to have abstained. Some of the court cards and jokers in each player's hand will have come from a different pack from the majority of preference cards, and will be clearly identifiable as votes against, even on the reverse side. Once the thirty-second time limit has elapsed, all of the cards which have been played are turned face up. If a majority of the cards played are *not* court cards or jokers, the motion passes. Otherwise, the motion fails.

7. *Payout*. If a motion fails, no payout is made and no cost is incurred by any player.

   If a motion passes, all players must pay a levy of £12.

   If a motion passes, *all players who voted in favour* receive the following payout:

   (a) A vote in favour with a card of a different suit to that of the issue under discussion receives the face value, in pounds, of the card played.

   (b) A vote in favour with a card of the same suit as that of the issue under discussion receives double the face value of the card played.

   (c) The player who plays the highest card in the suit representing the issue under discussion receives an additional £10 bonus.

   All votes against the issue in question receive nothing.

8. Discussion now moves to the next item on the agenda, as indicated by the next agenda card. If that card is face down, it is now turned face up. A three-minute negotiating session, followed by voting, takes place exactly as specified in rules 4–7. If the agenda

card is an ace, or if all twelve issue cards have been used, the session of the committee is at an end.

9. When the session ends, both packs of cards are reconstituted and reshuffled. A new session takes place, following rules 2–7.

HOW TO WIN ROLLING LOGS

With policy on four different issues to decide on, the way to win at Rolling Logs will be to try and buy support from players on some policies in exchange for your support on other policies. In each policy suit, there are only four preference cards which receive a positive payout when played to a winning vote. These are the seven, eight, nine and ten cards in the same suit as the issue in question. This will nearly always mean that there will not be a majority of players who favour any particular proposal when it comes up for discussion, yet the only way to make money is to push through proposals which give you some payout. You will know the order in which the policies are likely to be discussed, so the obvious thing to do is to approach someone in the negotiating sessions, offering to support a future policy vote, even if this yields no payout, or a loss, in exchange for support on your most lucrative policy.

Remember that, once you have played a card, it is gone forever. You must be relatively sure that you can play your high cards to good effect. This means simple deals like 'I'll do this for you, then you do that for me' will be regarded with deep suspicion by all concerned. Once I *have* done this, why should you actually go ahead and do that? You don't want to be suckered out of your good cards, and will need to find some way of keeping fellow conspirators on the hook. This may well involve a whole package of deals, with each side doing favours for the other, turn and turn about. People will be less inclined to double-cross you, because they still have something to lose. For example, you have a couple of high diamonds, an eight and a ten. The ten in particular is worth quite a lot to you if you can play it in a winning vote, since it is bound to be the highest card, and will win you a handy £10 bonus. If you play the card and the vote fails, however, you receive nothing, so you want to make sure that *this* vote, at least, is carried. You will try and recruit other people with high diamonds (who are also keen on industrial policy) but there will probably not be enough of them to ensure that the vote is carried. You will have to look further for support, and a likely direction is towards those people who will make a small loss if the vote is carried, but can be compensated in some other way. You will be looking for people with low diamonds, and the most obvious way of compensating them is a good old-fashioned cash handout. Another possibility is to look for people who have high cards in other suits, whom you can offer to support when their pet issue comes up for discussion in the future. Since you will not want to make a large loss on this trade, you will look for people who highly value a policy which you could support at little cost. Thus, if you want to find someone to support your education proposal, you should look at your hands for suits in which you hold medium cards, and then go off and try to do a deal with whoever holds a high card in that suit. Say you hold the six of spades. An ideal partner would be whoever holds the ten of spades, because you can support this person at no cost to yourself. Playing the six, and helping to pass a public works proposal, will cost you the £12 levy, and you will receive a payout of £12. If, when you find the person who holds the ten, it turns out that they also have the six of diamonds, you have a perfect trade on your hands, since they will be able to support you for nothing as well. To make sure that they keep their side of the bargain, if the vote on your issue comes after your support for them, you should consult the agenda and look for other issues on which you have similarly complementary preferences, so that, in a sequence of deals, you can help each other alternately. This will help you both to trust each other more.

You may well have high cards in two suits, and want to ensure a payout on both. This will probably mean doing deals with different people. You will find yourself conspiring with some players against others on some issues, and with other players against some on different issues. If you can get away with this, all well and good, but canny opponents may well try to tie in cooperation on a package of deals, in order to minimize their losses. Say, for example, you hold both the ten of diamonds and the ten of hearts. You fix up a deal with someone who holds the ten of spades, at no cost to yourself. You now go looking for a deal which makes sure you get a payoff for the ten of hearts. Your obvious partner for this may only have very low diamonds and spades, however, and be concerned at the prospect of projects being approved in these areas. In order to do a deal you may have to promise to hold back on your original deal. You will then have to decide which is the most likely to succeed, and go with that one.

A further complicating factor in all of this is the £10 bonus paid to the best card in a winning vote. This may well weaken the resolve of people who would otherwise be your natural allies. If you have the ten of diamonds, you might think that the player with the nine would be the obvious person to go and talk to. Not necessarily so : they may well want to bide their time until you're played your ten, in which case they will have the largest card in that suit, and stand to win a bonus. If you play your card in a losing vote, so much the better. This, in fact, is one player who may well try and lead you up the garden path.

The highest-card bonus also provides a way for people with really bad hands to make money (as well as by taking backhanders in exchange for votes). If all of the high cards in a particular suit have been played, even a relatively low card may still be the highest one left. This means that you could pick up a highest-card bonus with a card which would normally lose you money. If you can manage, towards the end of a session, to wangle a vote in favour of something for which the five you play is the highest card, you would end up £8 ahead, whereas a five played in any other winning vote would cost you at least £2. To try and arrange this, you should stir things up at the beginning of the game with the aim of forcing all of the high cards out in a single vote. The more this happens, the less bad a bad hand becomes, although you will still need to be extremely canny to make money out of it.

Your hand of preference cards also gives you a limited number of votes against issues. Deciding when to use these is obviously quite crucial. Just as you don't want to throw away your good cards voting for a proposal which fails, so you don't want to end up voting against something which succeeds; you just have to pay the levy without getting anything in return. If a vote looks like passing, you are better off jumping on the bandwagon and using a low card to vote in favour rather than voting against it regardless. Spotting when something is clearly going to pass is just as important as spotting when something is clearly going to fail.

This means that conspiring to vote against particular proposals will be every bit as important as conspiring to vote in favour of them. Such conspiracies are given an added dimension by virtue of the fact that some of the court cards and jokers will be clearly visible for all to see, coming from a different pack from the bulk of preference cards. Thus a particular deal may involve some of the participants playing these obvious jokers, to reduce the possibility of a double-cross. The disadvantage is that these obvious cards will alert the opposition, making them less likely to play and lose valuable cards. The decision to play, or agree to play, obvious or concealed jokers will therefore depend on whom you would most like to double-cross, and whom you trust the most. If you want to lure someone into throwing away their high cards, concealed jokers will be more effective. If you want to lure someone into voting against something which ultimately succeeds, you may want to agree to play obvious jokers, so that you can be sure that the bait has been taken before committing yourself.

It is quite possible that agreements to vote against some proposals will be coupled with agreements to vote in favour of others. You hold a high diamond and a high heart, for example, and do a deal with someone who has a high spade. You then go along to someone else, looking for a deal for your heart. Say the second person you approach has the next highest spade to that of your original partner. You may well now be asked to vote against the first spade proposal, double-crossing your original partner, leaving the way open for your new partner to get a bonus on the next public works proposal. The possibilities go on and on . . .

Two final matters to consider are the cards which are face down in the agenda, for which you cannot plan ahead, and the number of items which will be discussed in each session. The maximum number of items for an agenda is twelve, which gives you considerable scope for the sort of deals we have been discussing. Remember that the session is brought to a close if an ace is turned up, however. It is quite possible that one of the concealed agenda cards is an ace, bringing the session to an unexpected close. This will tend to undermine long-term deals, since you will never be sure whether your collaborators will ever have to fulfil their side of the bargain.

Any deal you make should contain some provision for the concealed agenda items. You might, for example, agree that deals only apply to those agenda items which can be seen in advance, with a free-for-all on all other matters. Or you might agree that the deal applies to all proposals, whether they can be foreseen or not. Such surprises may embarrass potential double-crossers, since they will be forced to show their hands sooner than they want. The prospect of such embarrassment should, in itself, do something to reduce the risk of being double-crossed. Thus, if you are feeling in a tricky mood, you should try only to make deals in relation to what is face up on the table, and leave yourself more scope for stabbing people in the back. If you are feeling distrustful, you should try to insist that deals apply to all proposals, whether or not they can be foreseen.

The main point of difference between this and the previous games is that the coalitions which form must change from issue to issue. The incentives for long-term cooperation are much weaker, and the way to make money will be to participate in a continually shifting system of alliances. The game will probably not split up into factions, since everyone will have an interest in cooperating with everyone else at some stage or other. The required mixture of conflict and cooperation is rather different since, as the ultimate strategy, it is quite possible to keep every one of the deals you make, and still end up the winner.

REALITY

Real politics is rarely concerned with a single issue, with the forces for and against arrayed in a relatively straightforward manner. Almost always, real politicians must balance their wishes on one issue with their wishes on other issues, given that they can't get what they want on all of them. Having done this, they must give something up in order to get what they most want, making concessions in less highly valued areas in exchange for support on their pet issue. This process is known as log-rolling, and is particularly important when no clear majority exists for certain proposals. Log-rolling is rather harder to observe in real life than some of the other things that we have talked about, because the cynical trading off of one issue against another is rather frowned upon. Notwithstanding this, log-rolling is clearly common practice, particularly in behind-the-scenes negotiations *within* particular groups. Furthermore it can often operate to the advantage of all participants. Indeed, in certain circumstances, nothing would ever get decided if logs weren't rolled from time to time.

The most explicit examples of log-rolling in national politics usually involve minority groupings of one form or another. Thus, in the absence of a majority party in the 1974-9 British parliament, we have seen some good examples in British inter-party politics. The Liberal Party, for example, has an enormous log which it has been trying, with little success, to roll at the other parties for some time. This is a proportional representation electoral system. When it became clear that Liberal support was going to be a great help in controlling the 1974-9 parliament, the Liberals disinterred proposals for their long-cherished electoral system. They tried to trade Liberal support on a range of other issues for a commitment to electoral reform from the Labour Party. If electoral reform had been agreed, the Liberals would, in exchange, have voted for measures in other fields which would, in normal circumstances, have been contrary to their policy, but which they regarded as far less important than a system of holding elections which would guarantee them a long-term future in British politics. The attempt met with little success because there was no other party which was worth trading with and which also did not regard electoral reform as one of the worst things which could happen. It should be clear from the game that the secret of log-rolling is to find a partner or group of partners who are not greatly harmed by helping you. In the end, a much more low-key package of proposals formed the basis of the 'Lib-Lab Pact'. On the other hand, the Scottish Nationalists were much more successful at rolling a rather large log in the direction of Westminster during the same parliament. Proposals for greater regional self-government were something which greatly concerned the Nationalists, but were of much less interest to the other parties, provided that things stopped short of total independence. Conversely, the Nationalists were much less concerned about the many other political issues which are central to Westminster party politics. These complementary preferences formed the basis of a quite productive (if implicit) deal, which led the Labour Party to make serious concessions in the direction of Scottish regional government. This was in the knowledge that to do so would encourage the Nationalists to keep Labour in power to enact some of the legislation which it was most concerned with.

Other examples of log-rolling at national level involve religious parties, or religious groupings within parties. It is not uncommon for religious parties in a number of European countries to be more concerned with religious affairs than they are with the other issues of national politics. They are thus well placed to trade support for other national parties in exchange for concessions on, for example, religious education in schools, divorce, contraception or Sunday observance. The recent history of Dutch politics provides a number of examples of this process at work.

The game shows that, for each participant, some opponents are easier to do deals with than others. If you feel strongly about some issue in which you are in a minority, you are in a good position if you feel weakly about another issue along with a majority of others. You can then go out looking for people to deal with, hoping to find someone who feels pretty apathetic about the issue which excites you, but is excited about the issue which leaves you cold. In these circumstances a deal is very easy to arrange. Sometimes, however, a group will find itself in a minority on all of the issues which concern it, and thus have nothing to offer anyone else by way of support. Log-rolling here is impossible, and other methods of getting your own way must be attempted. Ethnic minority groups are often in this position, particularly in societies where they are the object of discrimination. The emancipation which the minority group feels most strongly about is also the thing which most concerns the majority, so that there is no log-rolling deal whereby the minority can get its own way. Thus, while Scottish Nationalists could roll logs at Westminster, there was no prospect of Irish Nationalists successfully rolling logs in the Northern Ireland parliament. The Scottish Nationalists could succeed because Westminster did not really care very much about Scotland, one way or the other; Stormont, however, cared considerably about Ulster.

Thus log-rolling does take place in national politics although, for public relations reasons, it is rarely explicit. What goes on behind closed doors, however, is another matter. Many groups are divided all sorts of ways on the issues which divide them. Majorities frequently do not exist for *any* policies, so that, if no accommodation is arrived at, nothing at all will be done. A graphic example of this can be found in the recent history of Liverpool City Council. For some time, no party was able to command a majority in the council chamber. There were many local issues, furthermore, on which each party had a different opinion. In these circumstances, to avoid a total stalemate, log-rolling was almost the only answer. If deals were not arranged, any proposal put forward by one of the parties was automatically rejected by the other two. Since politicians think that the electorate frowns upon log-rolling, the only answer was to retreat into smoke-filled rooms and try to cobble together packages of issues which allowed the parties to trade support for each others' policies.

Individual parties or groups are themselves often split several ways on the issues, of course. This means that log-rolling is a necessary part of the process of coming up with a common party policy in the first place. The results of this can be easily observed in Britain during the annual policy-making jamborees of the main political parties, unions and pressure groups. Frequently, before any motions ever reach the conference agenda, the executive will sit down and produce a series of composite motions, ostensibly cobbling together the wishes expressed in the proposals of numerous local associations. This usually takes place behind closed doors, as does the discussion which leads to executive recommendations on each motion. One of the main reasons for this process is that, while each issue must be discussed on its individual merits in open session, complicated interactions between the various issues can be sorted out while the executive package is prepared. In general, the fact that logs are usually rolled behind closed doors is one of the most tantalizing aspects of the whole subject.

All types of log-rolling deal are, of course, highly susceptible to the double-cross. The actual issues are usually decided one after the other, so that someone must trust someone else, and must take the risk that the other will not deliver. In this respect, log-rolling is like the processes we have already discussed. There are two basic ways of attempting to reduce the risk of being cheated. On the one hand, everyone must try to build up some credibility if they want people to take them seriously in the future, and the best way to build up credibility is to keep your word, however painful this might appear in the short term. Since everyone will need to build up credibility, there is some chance that deals will stick. On the other hand, if log-rolling is always going to be necessary before any decision can be taken, it is possible that the participants will try to set up some formal institutions which ensure that deals are actually honoured. Government coalitions can do this quite easily when they carve up the cabinet, for example. When some parties are more interested in certain areas of policy than others, a log-rolling deal between parties to go into government can be partially secured by giving particular parties those ministries responsible for the policy areas which they are most interested in. This means that, in one simultaneous transaction, all parties gain some guarantee of a say in those future eventualities which they most want to control.

Log-rolling is a sophisticated process, however, and allows sophisticated double-crosses which are hard to thwart. Some of the best examples of this can be found in the field of international diplomacy. Imagine the world consisted of the five countries in the diagram on page 102, each suspicious of the other and looking for defence treaties. Victoria pulls off a sophisticated log-rolling double-cross by making deals with both Ruritania and Industria which appear to involve it in heavy commitments, but in fact cost Victoria next to nothing. Victoria says to Ruritania, 'I'll protect you against Industria, if you protect me from Atlantis.' Victoria then says to Industria, 'I'll protect you from Ruritania if you protect me from Flatland.' Victoria ends up with all sorts of protection from attack at almost no cost, since the two commitments which it has undertaken cancel each other out. The treaties appear to be equally advantageous to both sides, but Victoria needs to indulge in little expenditure protecting Ruritania from Industria precisely because it has also promised to protect Industria from Ruritania. It arranges a stand-off on this border, and gets quite a lot in return. If the mutual defence treaties are secret, no one need ever find out that they have been double-crossed. At the same time Victoria comes out ahead while appearing to be a good and faithful ally.

The politics of log-rolling is the politics of back-scratching, which is why it takes place in private, since back-scratching is rarely an edifying sight, however satisfying for the participants. Yet log-rolling is almost indispensable in many political situations, for without it many important decisions would never be taken. Both in the game and in real life, making a success of log-rolling is partly a matter of having something to trade, and partly a matter of skill. Even if you have nothing to trade, however, the final game should offer you hope . . .

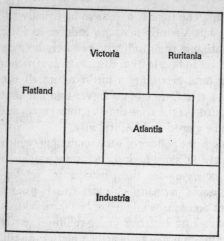

THE WORLD (SQUARE VERSION)

A game for five or more players. It should take from 1½ to 2 hours.

As in the previous game, the players are members of a committee, and each has strong feelings about a number of issues. This time, however, success or failure depends to a large extent on the ability to manipulate the rules of committee procedure. The incentive to come to arrangements with the others is still there, but there is also the possibility of going it alone and simply outwitting them.

EQUIPMENT

1. A bundle of money.
2. A pack of playing cards.
3. A blackboard, or large sheet of paper.
4. A watch.

RULES

1. Each player receives £100 from the Bank.
2. Each round of play represents one session of a committee. The players are all committee members. At the start of each round, a chairperson must be selected. One card is dealt to each player, and the player with the highest card chairs that round. If two or more players tie, further cards are dealt to them until the tie is broken.
3. At the start of each round, each player, including the player in the chair, must pay £40 to the Bank.
4. For each round, each player, including the person in the chair, has different ideas about the ways in which the committee's budget should be allocated between four important areas of expenditure. In order to decide these preferences, the pack of

cards is re-shuffled, and a card is dealt, face down, to each of the players in turn until the pack is exhausted. The player sitting on the right of the chair receives the first card. Some players will have one more card than others. As before, each suit represents a particular issue:

Hearts represent social security.
Clubs represent defence.
Diamonds represent industry.
Spades represent public works.

The players add up the face value of the cards they hold in each suit (court cards count zero). The total face value of cards a player holds in a particular suit represents the player's preferred expenditure, in millions of pounds, in this policy area. Thus a face value of twelve in hearts means that you would like to see £12 million spent this session on social security, while a face value of six in spades means that you would like £6 million spent on public works.

Players may, if they wish, show all or part of their hand to others, but will probably want to keep it secret at the start of the game.

5. Before each session of the committee gets under way, the chairperson must produce an agenda. This is a list of the various proposals which will be discussed, in order of discussion. Every player has the right to propose two motions, and does so by writing them on a piece of paper and handing it to the chair. The chair may not propose any motions. Each proposal must contain the name of the proposer, the issue to be discussed, and a proposed level of expenditure, in millions of pounds.

The player in the chair now has five minutes to prepare the agenda. This must include at least one proposal on each issue, unless no proposal at all has been made on a particular issue. It is quite permissible to place more than one proposal on a particular issue on the agenda. The choice of proposals, and the order in which they are placed on the agenda, is entirely at the discretion of the chair. At the end of the five-minute period, the player in the chair must write the agenda on the blackboard.

This must include the proposals chosen and the order in which they are to be discussed. Beside each proposal should be written the name of the proposer and the issue and level of expenditure contained in it.

Once the agenda is on the board, the committee is in session, and all private conversations between the players must stop at once.

6. Once the committee is in session, all remarks must be addressed to the chair. Any player holding a private conversation may be asked to stop. Once a player has been called to order in this way, any further disobedience of this rule may result in the offender being ejected from the meeting. Expelled players may not vote again in that session, although they continue to receive any payouts due to them. They may converse with other players only during a recess (see below). Any player talking to an ejected player may also be ejected from the meeting.

7. The proposals are discussed in the order in which they appear on the agenda, unless this order is changed by a procedural motion (see below). When a proposal comes up for discussion, the player in the chair reads it out, and asks if there is a seconder. If there is no seconder, discussion moves to the next item on the agenda. If there is a seconder, the proposal becomes a substantive motion before the committee. No other substantive motion may be discussed until the fate of the current substantive motion has been decided.

8. Once a motion has been proposed and seconded, the chair must ask for discussion. If there is no discussion, the motion is put immediately to the vote. If discussion is requested by any player, the chair must allow one speech for and one speech against the motion. At any stage in the discussion after this, the chair may decide to put the motion to the vote, unless there is an outstanding amendment or procedural motion (see below). The player in the chair may not vote on *any* motion, except in the event of a tie, when he or she has a casting vote.

9. At any stage during the discussion of the substantive motion, any player may propose an amendment to it. This amendment must make a proposal on the same issue as the substantive

motion, but may alter the proposed level of expenditure by up to £3m. If an amendment is proposed, the chair must ask for a seconder. If there is no seconder, discussion continues on the substantive motion as if no amendment had been proposed. If there is a seconder, the chair must ask for discussion of the amendment. One speech for and against the amendment must be allowed, after which it must be put to the vote. If the amendment is carried, it becomes the new substantive motion. If the amendment is defeated, discussion and voting continues on the original substantive motion. No more than two amendments are allowed on any single substantive motion.

10. Once an original or amended substantive motion on a particular issue is carried, no further discussion may take place in this session of the committee on that issue. The motion which has been carried becomes the policy of the committee for that session. The player in the chair writes this decision on the board, and removes any further proposals on this issue from the agenda.

11. Once a substantive motion has been carried or defeated, discussion moves on to the next proposal on the agenda, and proceeds according to rules 6–10. Additional proposals concerning issues for which policies have not yet been decided may be discussed.

12. The following *procedural motions* may be proposed by any player except the chairperson at any stage. Once a procedural motion had been proposed and seconded, it may be discussed before being put to the vote. Voting on procedural motions must take precedence over voting over any other motion or amendment. Procedural motions may not be amended. No more than one procedural motion may be under discussion at any one time. The procedural proposals which may be made are:

(a) A *recess*. If a proposal for a recess is carried, the committee goes into a three-minute recess, timed by the chair. During this recess, players may hold private conversations among themselves. This is the only circumstance during the period when the committee is in session that players may legally talk among themselves. Players may also converse with members of the committee who have been ejected. At the end of the recess, all private conversations must stop immediately, and all further remarks must be addressed to the chair.

(b) *An agenda motion.* Before any particular item on the agenda is discussed, a player may propose that an item further down the agenda be discussed first. If such a proposal is carried, the specified motion is discussed as if it were the next item on the agenda. Alternatively, a player may propose that voting on a particular motion be deferred until a specified point on the agenda has been reached. If the proposal is carried, discussion moves on to the next item on the agenda.

(c) *Next business.* At any time during the discussion of a particular substantive motion, a player may propose 'next business'. If this is seconded and carried, discussion of that item on the agenda is immediately terminated. Discussion moves on to the next item on the agenda, and a vote is never taken on the item which was terminated.

(d) *No confidence in the chair.* If a motion of no confidence in the chair is seconded and carried, the player in the chair must immediately stand down in favour of the proposer of this motion. If the no-confidence motion is carried, all players, except the new chairperson, must pay a forfeit of £10. If the no-confidence motion is defeated, the proposer must pay a forfeit of £10.

13. All votes are carried by an absolute majority of the players. All voting is by show of hands. The player in the chair may not vote on any matter, except to break a tie. Players may abstain in any vote.

14. Play continues until the agenda is exhausted. This will happen either when every proposal on it has been voted upon, or when a policy has been agreed on each of the four issues, when all other proposals will have been deleted. If no decision has been reached at this stage on one or more of the four issues, the chair may ask for further proposals on the outstanding business. Once this has been done, *one or two* proposals on each undecided issue must be taken, at the discretion of the chair. These pro-

posals are discussed and voted upon exactly as if they had been part of the original agenda. If there is still no decision on a particular issue after this has happened, then the expenditure on this policy area for this session is zero, and payouts are made accordingly.

15. *Payouts.* Once the agenda has been completed as described in rule 14, the committee session is declared closed, after which the members are paid off. Each player is paid on the basis of the closeness of each decision to his or her own preferred policy, as revealed in each hand of cards.

If the total expenditure decided by the committee on a particular issue is identical to a player's preferred expenditure, that player receives £20 from the Bank.

For every £1m. which the committee decision differs from the player's preference, £2 is deducted from this £20 payout.

If the player's preference differs from the committee decision by more than £10m., then the player must pay the Bank £2 for every additional £1m. deviation.

These payouts are made for each of the four issues, bearing in mind that, if no committee decision is reached, its expenditure on that issue is zero.

16. Once the payout has been made at the end of each session of the committee, a new session is convened, players pay another £40 to the Bank, and play commences as at rule 2.

HOW TO WIN AGENDA

There are four issues to be decided, and each of the players has different ideas on each of the four issues. Thus many of the tactics relevant to Rolling Logs will apply to Agenda. The deals and accommodations discussed in the previous chapter clearly represent one way of trying to win, although players must remember that the cost of not coming to a decision will be higher in Agenda, since each player must lay out £40 at the beginning of each session, regardless of the decisions which are arrived at. In addition, you must remember that payouts are made solely on the basis of the cards which a player holds in hand, regardless of how he or she has voted. Votes must therefore be used entirely in order to bring about your preferred outcome, although, as we shall see, this does not necessarily involve voting for every proposal which is close to one that you would like to see enacted.

The main difference between the two games is that deals are rather less important in Agenda, since there are many new procedural methods for coming out on top. The use which is made of these tactics depends upon whether you are chairing the committee or simply one of its members, and these two roles are best discussed quite separately.

THE CHAIR

Just because the chair has only a casting vote, and cannot propose motions, you should not conclude that it has little power. It should quickly become obvious that the power of the chair to decide upon the agenda for the discussions is extremely important. It will become apparent from playing the game that the order in which the proposals are discussed has a strong influence on which are accepted and which rejected. If there are three possible outcomes on a particular issue, and none of these has majority support, then the first proposal which is made on the subject will always tend to get rejected as its opponents join forces to defeat it. If this is the case, then putting an item high on the agenda will make it more likely to fail. As the end of the agenda approaches, the need for any decision rather than no decision will become more pressing in the minds of many of the players. The chances therefore increase for any proposal on an issue which has yet to be resolved. Other things being equal, you might therefore want to put favoured proposals relatively low on the agenda. This must be balanced against the possibility that some decision will already have been taken on the issue in question before your favoured proposal gets an airing.

Of course, if people suspect that something is going on, then they will try and outsmart you. If they think you are trying to out-manoeuvre them, this might increase the chances of items high on the agenda as your opponents try and pre-empt you. You, of course, will have the advantage that no one will know your preferences on any issue, so that they can never be *sure* of what you are trying to do. On balance, this probably makes fancy tactics by the chair worth the risks.

In the chair you have the power to select and reject proposals for discussion, provided that you include at least one item on each issue. Your selections can, of course, be modified by amendments, but since amendments can only change the substantive motion by up to £3m. at a time, the selection of proposals which you make will have some considerable influence on the result. You might decide to select items which are close to your own preferences, and to reject those which would lose you money. Alternatively, you may wish to include proposals which are not at all what you would like to see, either to confuse the committee as to your intentions, or in the hope that a ridiculous proposal will be rejected, paving the way for a later motion much closer to your own heart.

If people are trading with each other, you can attempt to control this by the way in which you select and order the items on the agenda. Most obviously, you can attempt to break up a particular cabal by including proposals, and putting them in an order, which makes it as hard as possible for the conspirators to do business with each other. For example, you could try to put those items proposed by the less trusting of the group late on the agenda, so that they have to make their commitments early, but only receive their rewards later. Alternatively, you could include a series of proposals which are as far as possible from the ones proposed by the cabal in the hope that, since consultation is not allowed once the committee is in session, you will throw the members into disarray.

One problem you will face with all of this is that you will need to make some guesses about the preferences of the members of the committee. The only real thing that you will have to go on will be the proposals made by each player. Making sense of these is far from easy, unless you think that the other players are naïve enough for you to be able to take their proposals at face value. Once they realize that it is very dangerous to be so frank in this sort of business, they will be trying to keep this information from you. From then on, their proposals will be designed to get what they want, which is quite a different thing from saying what it is. Sometimes they will be proposing quite the opposite (see below), and you will simply have to make what you can of what people say. In the end you'll just have to play your hunches when trying to root out the bluffers. Don't forget that, once they are playing the bluffing game with you, it is just as possible that they are telling you what they really do want as it is that they are telling you quite the opposite.

Having fixed the agenda you also have the power to run the meeting. You can, for example, select and reject speakers to further your own ends. The way in which you do this will depend on how you have doped out the opposition. The rules for accepting procedural motions may seem quite explicit, but you are bound to be able to find grey areas and loopholes to exploit where your decisions can be quite crucial. You should also be able to get away with a certain amount of rule-bending, since the main recourse that the players have against this is a motion of no confidence in the chair which, because of the possible penalties involved, they may be reluctant to attempt. Any gross fiddling should be left until towards the end of the session, when the costs of replacing you will just not seem worth it, however awful you become.

The great advantage that you retain throughout the period for which you remain in the chair is that you can be almost completely inscrutable, since no one will have any idea about your preferences. The other players have to make proposals and cast votes, but you are allowed to do neither, so that the other players are left with having to make what they can of your general conduct. The only time at which you have to commit yourself is when you are called on to make a casting vote. Casting this vote, by definition, decides the issue. Thus the only time at which you are forced to give away information, you can do yourself no harm. The issue on which you reveal information will thereby be decided, and cannot be further discussed. You may be faced with a tricky decision if you are called on to decide the fate of a motion which is close, but not very close, to the one you would most like to see passed. You will have to decide whether anything better is likely to succeed later on. Late in the proceedings you may have to cast your vote for something which you would much rather see defeated, because you cannot run the risk of no decision and zero expenditure. This is unless, of course, your preference on the issue in question is a very low level of expenditure, in which case you will want to be downright mischievous in order to prevent any decision being taken.

In conclusion, you should enjoy being in the chair, for the chairman's lot is quite a happy one. It is mainly happy precisely because you won't have to make proposals and vote and do all of those things which let people know what you're thinking, and encourage them to do you down. They'll *want* to do you down, but they won't know how to do it because they won't know what you want.

THE COMMITTEE MEMBERS

As a 'mere' member of the committee, you will be rather more active than the player in the chair, making proposals, speaking to motions, proposing amendments and voting. All of this activity provides your opponents with valuable information, and the more accurate information they have about you, the more likely they will be to confound you. One of your main concerns, therefore, will be to make sure that the information you involuntarily give away is as hard as possible to interpret accurately. As we have seen when discussing the role of the chair, you do not have to give information away on a plate. You know you are being watched for clues, so you can try and confuse people. They know you will be trying to confuse them, and they will take account of this. There is clearly a danger of things getting impossibly complicated, but remember that you do not really want the others to work out that you are trying to outsmart them. It may well be, therefore, that the simplest moves are the best, provided that you understand their consequences. If you seem to be playing a straightforward game, your opponents may conclude that you are being simple-minded, and therefore easy to outsmart. A general rule of thumb in this game is to look for clever reasons to make obvious moves.

Once you have seen your cards, you must make two proposals for the agenda. We have seen that you can either propose something which you want, or something which you don't want. Bear in mind that the authors of the proposals are identified on the agenda. You might not want to propose something and then vote against it, since this gives everyone a clear indication that you are playing a tricky game. You do not have to vote against something you don't want, however, provided you don't think your vote will make a crucial difference. If it is going to be defeated anyway, you can go ahead regardless and vote for a really awful proposal, not doing yourself any harm, and keeping all of your cards very close to your chest. This leaves the way open for you to propose, and support, a really ridiculous proposal in order to baffle the opposition.

There are two groups of people you might want to confuse. The player in the chair will see all proposals, so you can't avoid giving him *some* information, however confusing. You may want to make crazy proposals simply to give away no information at all, in the hope that these proposals will never appear on the agenda. This would mean that no one will know anything at all about what you want, not at all a bad position to be in at the start of the session. On the other hand, the player in the chair may try deliberately to confound you by including some of your wild proposals on the agenda, making it clear for all to see that you are playing it fast and loose. That's a risk you'll have to take, and even if everyone knows that that's the way you want to play it, they still won't know what you want. Barring this possibility, if you make a proposal it will be because you *want* to see it on the agenda. If it appears on the agenda, you will be providing information for the other players. Since you will be identified as the author of the proposal, your subsequent activity will give a good indication to the others of the way in which you are playing things. We have already seen that you can safely vote, on occasion, for things you don't want in order to give an impression of being straightforward. You might, however, want to do precisely the opposite, and vote against proposals which you have made yourself and would really like to see become committee policy. This can be particularly effective if you have a good idea that the proposal will be carried despite your opposition. The intention this time is the opposite of deception. You are deliberately trying to foster the impression of being a slippery customer, and might want to do this so that people won't believe what you say when you tell them the truth. In these circumstances you might induce them, in an attempt to confound you, to work for exactly what you want. Thus, while telling the truth for the sake of it can be very naïve and counterproductive, telling the truth for the right reasons can be rather sophisticated.

In short, the decisions you will have to make about what, precisely, to propose and how, precisely, to vote are as complicated as you care to make them. Once more, there are no hard-and-fast rules and you will just have to fly by the seat of your pants, bearing certain things in mind. Once more, simple moves are usually preferable to complex ones: they are more open to misinterpretation.

You have a whole range of additional tactics at your disposal as a 'mere' committee member, however. These arise from the whole range of procedural motions which you can try and make capital out of. Many of these can have important implications for your final payout. We have already seen that the order in which things are discussed can considerably affect the outcome. Several of the procedural motions represent methods for changing this order. Agenda motions move items up and down the agenda, while 'next business' scraps motions without a vote. The reasons why you might want to do this should by now be relatively obvious. You may not want to vote on a particular motion because you would rather conceal information about your preferences or your deviousness at a particular stage in the proceedings. If the player in the chair has called your bluff and tabled your crazy proposals, for example, you may want to get them deferred or scrapped. You can either do this personally (which itself will give information away) or through someone else (in which case you will have to take them into your confidence). On the other hand, you may have a possible deal which is being frustrated because of the order of the agenda, or your preferred motion may be riding too high or too low on the agenda for your liking once you have calculated what is going to happen to them in their present position. You may want to reduce the chances of a motion which you don't want to succeed by changing its position. In each case you will be giving something away by proposing the relevant procedural motion, but what precisely you are giving away may be far from obvious to the others.

All they will know is that you are up to something; it will still be necessary to work out what it is. Manipulating procedure can be a far more inscrutable method of getting your own way than making proposals and voting on more substantive matters.

The motion for a recess is a particularly important procedural device. You are not allowed to talk to the other members of the committee when it is in session, except through the chair, when *everyone* can hear. If you want to set up a private deal with some of the other committee members, or with the player in the chair, you will have to try and get a recess, in which you can hold private conversations with them. Once more, people will know that you are up to something but, if they are sensible, they will be suspecting everyone of being up to something anyway. Players who do not want you to fix something up will oppose you, but if they fail it gives them a chance to do some plotting as well, a fact which you should not overlook. Even though you would dearly like to go into a huddle with your fellow conspirators, you may decide that the opposition is in greater disarray than you are, and press on regardless, even opposing a recess.

Finally, the no-confidence motion gives you the chance to throw out the incumbent chairperson. Remember that the successful proposer of a no-confidence motion takes the chair if it succeeds, but pays a penalty if it fails. Everyone else pays a penalty if the motion succeeds. You might want to propose no confidence in the chair because you would like to take the chair yourself, although you would be wise to make sure that you have enough support before you try this. You might do so even if you don't particularly want the chair for yourself, but because you want to get rid of a particularly bad or biased chairperson before you suffer too much damage. Having decided on a coup, you might as well be the one who makes the proposal, since you save £20 that way by winning £10 instead of losing it. The decision to support a motion of no confidence must take into account the likely conduct in the chair of the new challenger and the costs and benefits of allowing the incumbent to continue in office. Even if you don't like the way they are doing things, you may feel that the challenger would be worse or that the benefits are not worth incurring the £10 levy if a take-over occurs. Of course, during a recess, the proposer of the motion may offer to help you with this expense in exchange for your vote.

In conclusion, it is clear that the things which you must take into account when trying to win Agenda are sufficiently complicated and imponderable that it is not possible to work out what best to do with anything approaching certainty. The chance element in this game is not automatically built in, as it is in some of the others, since any hand you are dealt can be a good one. What is unpredictable is the way in which the players will interact with one another. In the end, you will just have to do something and back a hunch; the important thing is to do it for the right reason.

REALITY

We have already discussed log-rolling, and log-rolling will obviously be a very important ingredient of this sort of wheeling and dealing in committee. In addition to this, Agenda sets out the crucial importance of procedure when it comes to getting your own way when confronting a small group of highly rational opponents in a relatively formal setting. Readers who have sat on committees themselves will be well aware of the critical importance of a sound grasp of procedure. Important matters of policy are often settled by apparently obscure wrangles over apparently irrelevant matters of procedure which seem indescribably petty to the innocent bystander. Issues can be won or lost according to the way in which the participants play the procedural game.

Once more we find that power is not quite what it seems. Consider the role of the chair. It is very common for this person to play no part at all in the discussion of substantive issues (indeed it is often considered quite improper for them to do anything else). Usually the chair has only a casting vote in the event of a tie, and superficially has little formal power, serving simply to keep the discussion under control by applying a few basic procedural rules. This apparent impotence is, of course, belied by the tremendous significance given to the struggle between the interested parties on many committees to control the chair. Procedural rules can be used with devastating impact. Consider, for example, a local government housing committee, split three ways over the alternative uses of a particular piece of land. One group would most like to see the council build homes for sale, after that it would like to have homes for rent, and after that, private housing. For another group, homes for sale is the worst possible outcome; it would rather have pure council or private housing, and of these alternatives prefers council development. The third group most wants private housing and least wants council housing, seeing homes for sale as a compromise between these two. The three groups therefore list the outcomes in order of preference as follows:

	Group A	Group B	Group C
First	Council sale	Council rent	Private
Second	Council rent	Private	Council sale
Third	Private	Council sale	Council rent

(Readers are free to re-label these groups as they see fit.) If the housing committee must come to a decision on the fate of a particular piece of land, the outcome in this instance is entirely dependent on the procedures adopted. If all of the councillors are relatively naïve, saying what they think and voting for what they want, then the first proposal which is made always gets defeated by a coalition of the other two groups. This leaves a straight fight between the remaining alternatives. Precisely which outcome emerges as successful depends on which proposal was made first and rejected. If council homes for sale is proposed by group A, it gets defeated, leaving a majority in favour of council homes for rent. If council homes for rent is proposed first, it gets defeated, leaving a majority for private housing. If private housing is proposed by group C, then it gets defeated, leaving a majority for council homes for sale. Such naïve councillors would be easy to outwit. If one group wakes up to what is going on, and tries to play the system, they will certainly not start by proposing what they want. If what they want appears high on the agenda, they will do what they can to move it down, postponing a decision until at least one of the alternatives has been rejected. Better than that, they will try and get the right proposal discussed first. Thus group B councillors, who want homes for rent, should dream up some pretext for proposing that homes for sale is discussed first. This way, they greatly increase the chances that the eventual outcome will be homes for rent. Obviously group A councillors will try and oppose this, since putting their baby first makes sure that it goes out with the bathwater. If everyone is that smart, they will all be sitting on their hands, making no substantive proposals and trying by whatever procedural means they can to get someone else's proposal discussed first.

It's possible to be smarter still, however. Imagine a group B councillor who has worked all of this out and starts putting himself in the other's shoes. He sees that everyone is holding out on making a proposal, and thinks about what happens if he just goes on and proposes what he wants regardless. If everyone is naïve his proposal will be defeated, and private housing will beat homes for sale. But everyone is not naïve, or they would all be jumping in with two left feet. If they are a little bit smart, smart enough to hold back, then proposing what you want is actually rather a clever thing to do. If homes for rent is defeated and private housing prevails, someone else stands to get the last thing they want. Group A puts private housing right at the bottom of its list. They will surely not stand by and let this happen, when there is something that they can do about it. What they can do is vote for homes for rent right away, guaranteeing their second choice rather than their third one. So if everyone is being smart and holding back, it's even smarter to get in there, because someone will support you to keep out their last choice. Incidentally, you will notice that, by being super-smart, you are doing exactly what you would have done if you'd been really naïve, just jumping right in there. If *everyone* had been naïve, this would have spelt disaster; it now works because you can take advantage of the fact that the others think they are being smart.

Obviously, the power vested in the chair to set the agenda is very important in this sort of situation. It can be used to considerable advantage even when it is possible for the others to fiddle around with the order in which things are discussed. Even though procedural motions might change the agenda, we have just seen that making sure that people don't realize you are being sophisticated can often make all of the difference. Trying to change the agenda is a sure way of signalling this, and thus of alerting your opponents that you have something up your sleeve. By fixing the agenda in advance, whoever occupies the chair can at least flush all of this out into the open. We have seen also, however, that being smart but not smart enough can be very dangerous, since you are as open to exploitation as someone who is completely naïve. Thus the power of the chair to organize business is only an asset as long as you have the measure of committee members. Once you get out of your depth, trying fancy strategies can land you in serious trouble.

It's not always as complicated as this, of course. Often you will find yourself in a minority facing majority opposition, or in the majority yourself. When this is true you don't have to bother with some of the subtleties necessary to win this game. This does not mean that situations calling for sophisticated manipulation of the rules of committee procedure occur only in a peculiar minority of cases. Often you will not know who wants what, even if there is, in fact, a majority for some proposal or other. Until you know where the majority is, you will have to play things very cannily. Many other times, particularly in the policy-making bodies of political parties, local councils, union executives or whatever, there will be a wide range of options on the cards at the beginning of a particular debate, each with its own supporters. These options may well end up being boiled down to a clear choice between two alternatives, but the process of boiling them down can involve some very subtle manoeuvres. Thus, while many of those involved will see two clear choices, the real decisions will already have been made. Very often these problems are resolved on the basis of rather odd-looking disputes over rather obscure points of procedure. Obviously disputes over the nature of trade union rule books, the methods of conducting particular items of business and the formation of composite motions by the executive of a particular organization are often hotly contested because they are not just about the best way of doing things. They are the real disputes which decide the winners and the losers.

It is very difficult to know where to look for hard evidence that real politicians actually think like this. The same actions can always be taken for a number of reasons, and no one is, as yet, very good at reading minds. It is not insignificant, however, that strongly disputed issues very often get bogged down in procedural wrangles and that the foundations for many of the coups, counter-coups and revolutions in our institutions are laid with the help of obscure sections in little used rule-books.

Games are games and politics is, of course, politics. Many readers will no doubt be appalled at my apparently flippant equation of the two. However, as I said in the Introduction, this book is not about the great issues of politics, it is about the means to these ends. In the real world it is impossible to separate means from ends quite so simply. Many horrible things have been done in the name of great causes, and some of these means have obviously distorted, or even confounded, the relevant ends. Mere mortals, however, cannot study everything at once. One of the ways in which we can try to come to grips with a difficult and complicated world is to draw distinctions which we know to be arbitrary and unrealistic in the hope that, by holding some things constant, we can gain some intellectual purchase on the others. This is one justification for the rather cynical and amoral tenor of this book. Ethics and ideals have been steadfastly ignored in an attempt to prize open the Pandora's Box of political strategy. Good politicians may well be good, but they are also politicians. Politics is about power, and power is about getting your own way, *whatever* that might be.

Above all, of course, games should be fun to play. If you do not enjoy playing these games, even a little bit, then they have failed. For this reason, it's best not to be too serious about them, since the proof of the pudding is in the eating. There are lots of games around, however, so why should you waste your time playing political games, when you could be having lots of fun, and maybe even making some money, playing One-eyed Jack or Kansas City Lowball? The answer, if you need one is that in politics, games and the real world come quite close together. Games are about means and nothing else, since the goals which the players must achieve are almost always arbitrary and irrelevant. Each game represents a particular type of conflict between a group of calculating and motivated players. Every game represents a particular puzzle, a particular structure of human interaction, and these structures can recur in several areas of social life. Thus Poker is Poker, but we *can* gain some insight into other conflicts by talking about them as if the participants were playing Poker. Any showdown between highly rational politicians, when each is trying to work out whether the other is bluffing, will be a little bit like Poker. It does make sense to look at a hijacking, a kidnapping or an international incident in these terms. Alternatively, at least one author has produced an interesting and provocative study of guerrilla warfare by likening it to Go, the ancient Chinese game of encirclement. It is, therefore, no accident that the language of games forms part of the language of politics, with its gambles and its gambits, its bids and its bluffs, its races, its rounds and its lotteries. People can become fascinated with politics for the same reason that they can become fascinated with games. Both are more or less stylized mechanisms for achieving a certain set of objectives with a limited set of resources when others are trying to do the same thing.

Students of politics have even developed a theory of games, most of which bears very little relation to this book. While the games that you have played have nothing to do with game theory, one of the basic ideas of this theory might help us to understand something about them. This is the classification of games into three basic types, games of pure cooperation, games of pure conflict, and games which are a mixture of the two.

In games of pure conflict, known in the trade as 'zero sum games', everything which is won by any of the players must be lost by the others. If two people play, everything I win, you lose; everything I lose, you win. A very large number of gambling games, spectator sports and games played simply for fun fall into this category. Examples include Poker, Chess, Football, Boxing and Ludo. In the real world, things are rarely so clear cut, but there are some political games of pure conflict, including presidential elections and some games of war (although not nuclear war, which everyone can lose). More often than not, however, in real-life games some of the outcomes are better for all concerned than others. People have some incentive to cooperate and avoid the outcome which no one wants.

Games of pure cooperation, which are at the other extreme, are rather more rare. Even when everyone wants the same thing, however, communication problems can sometimes make cooperation difficult to achieve. A gaming example of this is Charades, where everyone is trying to guess the charade, the actor is trying to help them, and there are no real winners or losers. Everyone wins or everyone loses, and Charades is only a game at all because the person doing the mime is not allowed to speak. A real-life cooperation game arises when you become separated from a friend in a busy shopping area. You want to find each other, but cannot communicate. You must try and work out what your friend will do, what they think you will do, and so on. The game would disappear completely if you both had two-way radios since, unless you decide to play Hide and Seek, no conflict at all is involved. Real-world examples include two generals trying to unite their armies under radio silence, two civil servants trying to give the same answers to an investigative committee, or two criminals trying to produce the same alibi under questioning.

Most real-life games, and certainly most political games, contain a mixture of conflict and cooperation. This combination defines the final category of games, which are usually referred to as 'mixed-motive' or 'variable-sum' games. Gaming examples of mixed-motive games are rather rare since most people seem to prefer clear-cut winners and losers. Team games, however, can often produce mixed motives *within the team*, although not in the game as a whole. The individual player wants the team to win, but also wants to do well personally. Thus a team of runners or cyclists may pace each other; if they do not, the team will stand no chance of winning, but each will also want to beat the other members of the team when it comes to the sprint finish. At the start of the race, there is almost pure cooperation, at the finish it is pure conflict; somewhere in between there is a mixture of the two. The selfish footballer is also playing a mixed-motive game, wanting his team to win, of course, but wanting to get all the goals himself. The crunch comes when he is faced with deciding whether to pass the ball to someone with a better chance of scoring, or to press on himself. The team does better if he passes, but he might do better if he hangs on. Political examples of mixed-motive games are legion; most of politics consists of balancing mixed motives. One graphic example should illustrate the point. Consider two heads of state contemplating waging nuclear war on one another. Each would most of all like to beat the other and rule the world. If war is declared, however, the other side might retaliate, and the ensuing holocaust make both worse off than they were before they started. Each therefore has an incentive to cooperate with the other to avoid the destruction of the planet, since, if they fail, there will be no world to rule. Both motives operate simultaneously, pulling the actors in different directions.

The games in this book are mixed-motive games for most of their duration. Towards the end of the game, conflict tends to assert itself because there is, after all, only one winner. Until this point has been reached, the games have been designed so that no player can stand much of a chance of winning without some form of cooperation with some of the others. These games are not, of course, unique in this respect, although this combination of motives is much more common in real life than at the gaming table. The board game Diplomacy is a good example of a game with a similar structure, as are one or two other games of strategy which are won by cooperating to successively eliminate the other players.

Where the games in this book do differ from nearly all others is that the players, if a majority of them agree, may change most of the rules. This possibility only really arises with games with mixed motives since, in a game of pure conflict, the incentives for groups of players to cooperate at all, much less over changing the rules, are negligible. The rule allowing the rules to be changed is particularly appropriate to political games, since one of the main things which politicians do is make up and change rules. Rule-changing games are rather more complicated than most others, because the players can never be completely sure which precise game they are playing. Some rule changes can even change the whole character of the game, transforming it, for example, from a game with mixed motives to a game of pure conflict. The changes which are produced from modifications to the rules can often be quite unexpected. Sometimes quite dramatic-looking modifications can have no real effect at all on what is going on, and sometimes apparently innocuous modifications can be fundamental. Thus it is in the world of real politics, with a tremendous upheaval, such as the granting of independence to a colony, leaving everyone feeling better but still playing the same game, while a further innocuous amendment to the constitution transforms the president from a puppet to a potential dictator. Being able to play the rule-changing game is a fundamental political skill. Plotters and schemers look for innocent-looking changes with far-reaching consequences, while those trying to fob off demands for fundamental reform look for spectacular changes which make no real difference.

The games in this book are also exercises in bargaining and strategy. Because cooperation is essential to success, bargains must be struck which lay down the limits and intended consequences of this cooperation. When each game starts, no deals are enforceable. When deals are both essential and unenforceable, two things encourage you to keep your side of the bargain. The first is the threat of reprisals, while the second is your need for credibility. Some reprisals are possible in these games. Opponents can threaten never to deal with you again, or to concentrate on forcing you out of the game. Other reprisals, such as direct attacks or fines on recalcitrants, are prohibited by the Fundamental Laws of Nature since, once started, there is no knowing where they might stop. It is the need for credibility, however, which will have tended to keep you on the straight and narrow. Since you must cooperate to win, you will have no chance of winning if nobody will cooperate with you, and nobody will cooperate with you if you are an inveterate double-crosser. You stick to some deals because you need to make more deals. Building up and maintaining credibility is, of course, another fundamental political skill, and a large part of political debate concerns the credibility or otherwise of the participants. Thus politicians try to keep their election pledges because they want people to believe the next ones, while they try and undermine their opponents by placing great stress on inconsistencies between promises and performance.

Finally, the games are strategic because, if you want to win, you must take account of what your opponents are likely to do, what they are likely to think that you are likely to do, and so on.

This sort of calculation can go on forever with unpredictable and occasionally disastrous consequences. The classic example of this is the game of Showdown, played between the two fastest guns in the West, who have just bumped into each other on Main Street. Their trigger fingers tense and everyone dives for cover. As a matter of fact, neither of them wants to play Showdown, since both want to go home to their new 'constant companions'. *Really* they are playing a game of pure cooperation, which has no name because it never ends up getting played. Each knows he wants to go home. Each knows the other wants to go home. But each has a worm in the brain because he can't be absolutely sure that the other guy is sure that he is sure that that is how it is. Each thinks, 'I want to go home, but does *he* know that? I know he wants to go home, but does he know I know that? Even if he knows both those things, does he know that I know that he knows them? If there is any doubt in his mind about what I want to do, what I think he wants to do, what I think he thinks I want to do, and so on, he will have to shoot me first, in case I shoot him. THEREFORE, even though it is the last thing I want to do (short of dying) I have got to shoot him; there's absolutely no choice.' Someone *always* gets shot, because *no one is ever sure.*

That's in the films. In reality lives are saved because the participants decide that it is either too difficult or too dangerous to even consider the implications of these strategic possibilities. They abandon calculation and play hunches. Even in some of these games, trying to calculate all of the angles is no substitute for developing a feel for what is going on. The good politician succeeds as much by intuition as by analysis, because strategy is as much an art as a science.

More About Penguins
and Pelicans

Penguinews, which appears every month, contains details of all the new books issued by Penguins as they are published. It is supplemented by our stocklist, which includes almost 5,000 titles.

A specimen copy of *Penguinews* will be sent to you free on request. Please write to Dept EP, Penguin Books Ltd, Harmondsworth, Middlesex, for your copy.

In the U.S.A.: For a complete list of books available from Penguins in the United States write to Dept CS, Penguin Books, 625 Madison Avenue, New York, New York 10022.

In Canada: For a complete list of books available from Penguins in Canada write to Penguin Books Canada Ltd, 2801 John Street, Markham, Ontario L3R 1B4.

In Australia: For a complete list of books published by Penguins in Australia write to the Marketing Department, Penguin Books Australia Ltd, P.O. Box 257, Ringwood, Victoria 3134.